Applying Secure Base Leadership principles to coaching practice...

...to unleash potential and co-create the conditions where people can Play to Thrive.

IMD

Real learning
Real impact

Chemin de Bellerive 23
P.O. Box 915
CH-1001 Lausanne
Switzerland
Tel: +41 21 618 0111
www.imd.org

ISBN 978-2-940485-77-2

Dedicated to:

TPMO: The high-performing, secure base team: 20 years and counting...

Nils, Michael, Eric, Jorge, Alastair, Philippe, Steve & Susan

And all the secure base people and coaches I am privileged to know

Bless you for who you are and the work that you do

to challenge what is and inspire what could be.

"Our deepest fear is not that we are inadequate. Our deepest fear is that we are powerful beyond measure. It is our light, not our darkness that most frightens us. We ask ourselves, 'Who am I to be brilliant, gorgeous, talented, fabulous?' Actually, who are you not to be? Your playing small does not serve the world. There's nothing enlightened about shrinking, so that other people won't feel insecure around you. We are all meant to shine, as children do. We were born to make manifest the glory of the God that is within us. It's not just in some of us; it's in everyone. And as we let our own light shine, we unconsciously give other people permission to do the same. As we're liberated from our own fear, our presence automatically liberates others."

Marianne Williamson
Author, Speaker & Spiritual leader

PRAISE FOR SECURE BASE COACHING

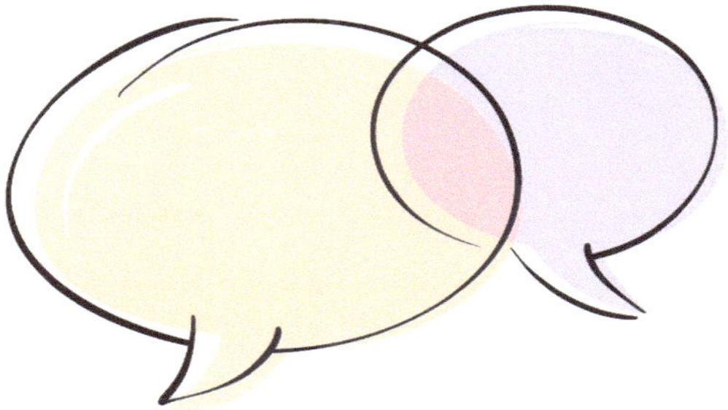

I strongly believe high-performance is a combination of results and the right behaviours creating these results. To unlock the potential of people, teams and organizations, the combination of Caring, Daring and Sharing are equally important. That's why we invest in all our colleagues, focussed on these three core behaviours. And since we are keen to create lasting impact, our approach is leader-led supported by a network of trained internal ambassadors.

Karin Van Baardvijk
CEO, ROBECO

As a coach, your role is to provide people with what they need, not always what they ask for. To achieve this, you need to establish a safe space by being a secure base for the coachee so they can be vulnerable and discover new possibilities.

Eivind Slaaen
Head of People & Culture Development,
Hilti Corporation

IMD's purpose involves challenging what is and inspiring what could be, which we pursue through the programs we offer but also in the insights and frameworks that we develop. One of the key ideas developed by IMD faculty over the years is the notion of secure base and its associated principles of caring, daring and sharing – all of which are very relevant for coaches and coachees. Through creating secure connections and encouraging coachees to step beyond their comfort zones, coaches can support leaders in unleashing their potential to the benefit of the individual, team and organization.

Jean-Francois Manzoni
Professor of Leadership and Organizational Development, IMD
President, IMD (2017-2024)

PRAISE FOR SECURE BASE COACHING

Climbing mountains with a disability has taught me that in order to achieve one's true potential it is invariably necessary to draw from the strength, knowledge and wisdom of others.
The pillars of secure base leadership are paramount to this principle. In changing and uncertain times, it is the role of the coach, through caring, daring and sharing, to inspire and encourage so that others may flourish and succeed.

Jamie Andrew
Motivational Speaker, Author,
Mountaineer, Quadruple Amputee

Secure Base Coaching provides a conceptual roadmap and practical guidance that will benefit both coach and coachee in their development, impact and effectiveness.

Duncan Coombe
Organizational Culture V.P, Professor, Author, C-Suite Coach

Life is best when we mindfully coach the growth of each other through a series of daring ventures to unleash the hidden potential that we all have. The best way to embrace this dynamic of sustainable growth is by offering an environment of Secure Base, like a caring belayer supporting the effort of the daring climber.

Jean-Pierre Heiniger,
mountaineer, OD Consultant & Leadership Coach

PRAISE FOR SECURE BASE COACHING

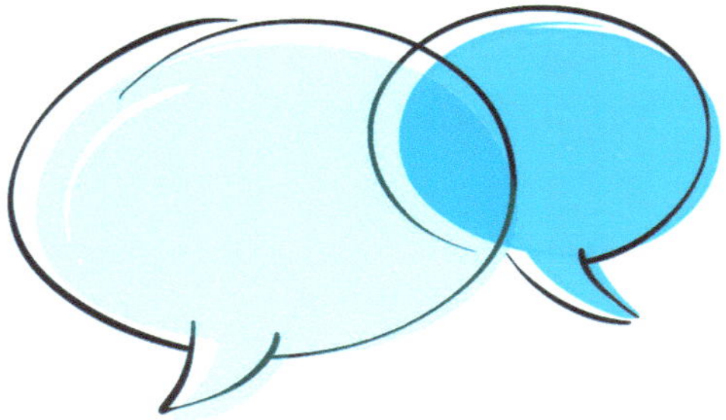

When leaders embody secure base coaching, they create a positive environment, focus on the future, invest time in developing others, show empathy and self-awareness, and encourage others to take responsibility and try new ideas. This approach unleashes the potential in each individual to grow, contribute, impact, and help organizations thrive. It is vastly different from old-school, command-and-control, fear-based management techniques, which sadly still exist in the corporate world. Secure base coaching provides the warmth and respect that everyone yearns for and can enjoy giving to their teams, enabling them to thrive and leaving a positive mark on their careers and our organizations for the future.

Anthony Venus
Founder, Luminous & Partner, CEO Coaching International

When we as leaders want to play to thrive, it's not about telling others "From now on we start playing to thrive, let's go". No questions, no discussions, I said so, you go. This won't work. It's rather about creating the secure base and coaching our team, so that the team sees us as role models of both caring and daring, creating space to ask questions, raise concerns, think together and together come to understand the true benefits of playing to thrive.

Anna Evstropova
Global Leadership Programs Director, SANOFI

Even though nobody likes perfect people, we spend a lot of effort looking strong, in control, unfaced. Yet, if we want to grow and develop, we need to be willing to be vulnerable and share our hopes and fears. This is why secure-base coaching is so important.

Robert Hooijberg
Professor of Organizational Behaviour, IMD

PRAISE FOR SECURE BASE COACHING

Secure Base Leadership, is, to my mind, the most accessible and universal model to help leaders inspire the courage that powers organizational growth. When we as coaches model caring and daring through Secure Base Coaching, we not only create a safe space where they can challenge deeply held beliefs, but also demonstrate how they can do the same for their people.

Katherine Armstrong
Founder: Cusp, Senior Executive Coach & Consultant

Being a secure base to another person comes with a great responsibility. There is a dilemma that coaches (and leaders) often fall into: do I coddle or do I push? In the long run, neither is effective. It's a false dilemma. Effective coaches nurture and challenge simultaneously. Secure base leadership and coaching starts by recognizing the humanity behind every person in the room.

Peter Meyers
Founder & CEO, Stand & Deliver
Author, Speaker, Theatre Director

If there is one certainty in an increasingly turbulent world, it's this: Disruption, uncertainty and change are coming our way. The SBL principles shared in this playbook build strong relationships, create authenticity & trust, and drive higher levels of performance. We need secure base coaches who can develop secure base leaders who show humility. Being humble does not mean thinking less of yourself. Rather, it means thinking of yourself less. Secure bases value people. They show us not who we are, but who we might become.

Terry Small,
The "Brain Guy"

PRAISE FOR SECURE BASE COACHING

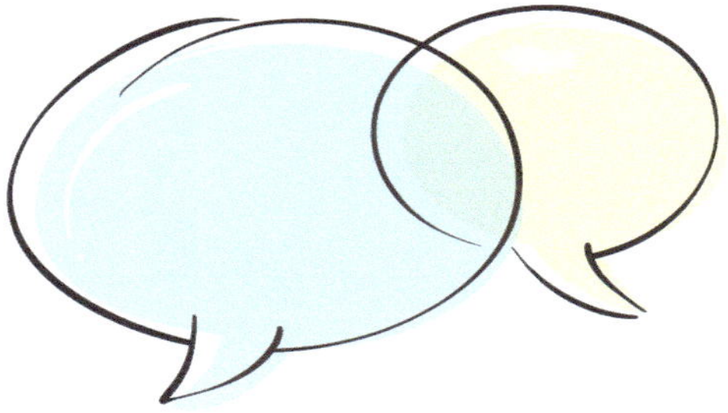

At our core, we believe that leaders as secure base coaches are pivotal in unlocking potential. Through our coaching ambassador program, we cultivate leaders who are skilled in creating environments where team members can 'play to thrive'. The techniques shared in this playbook drive both individual growth and foster a culture of continuous improvement and innovation.

Carsten Diederich,
Head Deal-to-Cash Operations, ALPIQ

Before we can effectively connect with others, we need to be fully connected to ourselves first. Secure Base Coaching offers practical tools to lead from a place of inner knowing and stillness. Only from that place can we truly connect to the people around us, in order to thrive as a leader. Whatever our functional role may be. I would have loved to have this guide earlier on in my career. Secure Base Coaching tools enable people to increase their awareness, so their actions become more intentional. This is, I believe, the surest way for people and organizations to thrive.

Maartje Jäckel MSc,
Wandering Coaching & Development,
the Netherlands

A leader who serves as a secure base provides a foundation of trust and support, enabling individuals to take risks and explore their true potential. Through the power of coaching, this secure environment fosters personal and professional growth, empowering people to thrive and perform at their best.

Frank Schönenberger
HR Business Partner, Julius Bär
COO Managing Director

PRAISE FOR SECURE BASE COACHING

Adhering to secure base leadership principles is fundamental in my coaching practice and allows me to establish a safe coaching context and contribute to powerful coaching journeys. Staying calm and listening attentively builds trust and openness, while encouraging risk-taking fosters the coachee's growth through innovation and resilience.

Silke Mischke
Senior Advisor, Co-program Director, IECC, IMD

Leaders can play an immensely valuable part in unlocking the potential within teams, creating 'play to thrive' environments and acting as secure base coaches when implementing the frameworks and techniques shared in this playbook.

Nicolas Crettenand
CEO Hydrospider @ALPIQ

Grounding oneself through practicing awareness opens the possibility to coach from a much wider place; the unbounded space of the mind. The coach's ego, with all its feelings and emotions, naturally remains in the background and we can then coach at ease with ourselves. This playbook makes it much easier to care, dare and share.

Erick Rinner
IMD Executive-in-Residence, Mind Training Instructor & Coach

CONTENTS

WHY THIS, WHY NOW ?

How does a lobster grow?

The metaphor of how a lobster grows beautifully illustrates the power of secure base coaching.
A lobster must shed its hard shell to grow, a process that leaves it vulnerable but is essential for its development.
If it sheds its shell in the open it will be eaten. Therefore, it needs to find a a rock or a cave where it feels safe enough to shed its shell and grow a new one. Similarly, secure base coaching provides a safe and supportive environment where individuals can shed their protective layers of fear and self-doubt. This coaching approach encourages them to embrace vulnerability, explore new possibilities, and grow beyond their perceived limitations. By fostering trust and safety, secure base coaching enables people to navigate periods of discomfort and uncertainty with resilience, ultimately emerging stronger and more capable. Just as the lobster develops a new, larger shell, individuals supported by secure base coaching can expand their potential and achieve greater inner growth.

WHY THIS, WHY NOW ?

This 'playbook' was born out of requests as to how to coach people to 'play to thrive' in increasingly adverse environments and working with coaches and leaders to transform people and cultures from within.

Secure base coaching plays a crucial role in helping individuals, teams, and organizations navigate the escalating stress and anxiety brought about by modern political, technological, environmental, and societal challenges. By providing a foundation of trust and safety, it enables people to explore their potential and overcome obstacles without fear of judgment or failure. This approach fosters resilience, creativity, and adaptive thinking, empowering individuals, teams and organizations to take risks, to innovate and perform at their best despite external pressures.

Central to this process is the importance of human-to-human connection, which reinforces empathy, understanding and collaboration. Organizations that embrace secure base coaching can cultivate a culture that enhances well-being AND drives sustainable success in an increasingly complex world.

Far from exhaustive, the exercises and questions included here are offered as a starting point; a source of stimulation and inspiration for coaches to become even more familiar with secure base principles, to apply them in their coaching sessions, and to explore secure base questions of their own.

WHAT ARE THE ROOTS OF THIS APPROACH ?

Secure Base Coaching is a transformative approach grounded in key psychological theories and practices that aim to unleash human potential. This method draws its foundational roots from the work of John Bowlby, Mary Ainsworth, Carl Rogers, and Sir John Whitmore, integrating their insights to create a robust guide for personal and professional development. It is informed by the work of Kohlrieser, Goldsworthy & Coombe in their award-winning book, Care to Dare, which leveraged Coombe's PhD research.

John Bowlby's concept of a "secure base" originates from his pioneering work in attachment theory, emphasizing the importance of a trusted and supportive figure in fostering an individual's sense of security and capacity for exploration. Mary Ainsworth's work illustrated how secure attachment patterns in early life shape our ability to form healthy relationships and face challenges with resilience.

WHAT ARE THE ROOTS OF THIS APPROACH ?

Carl Rogers developed the person-centred approach, which posits that individuals possess an inherent ability for self-directed growth. Rogers emphasized the significance of empathic understanding, unconditional positive regard, and congruence in creating a nurturing environment where people are more likely to trust their inner experiences and pursue their true selves.

The actualizing tendency, another concept introduced by Rogers, is the inherent drive within every individual to grow, develop, and realize their full potential. This tendency is a fundamental aspect of human nature, fostering resilience, creativity, and the ability to overcome obstacles, guided by one's own values and experiences, in the pursuit of becoming the best version of oneself.

A secure base coach operates from this understanding in co-creating the conditions of radical acceptance that encourage the coachee to stretch to fulfil potential.

WHAT ARE THE ROOTS OF THIS APPROACH ?

Sir John Whitmore articulated the essence of coaching as unlocking human potential. Whitmore's approach underscores the role of the coach in providing a supportive, non-judgmental space that encourages individuals to explore their capabilities, set meaningful goals, and achieve personal growth.
Secure Base Coaching synthesizes these perspectives, offering an holistic coaching framework that empowers people to navigate their personal and professional journeys with confidence and clarity.

Coaching is unlocking a person's potential to maximize their own performance.

Sir John Whitmore,
1937-2017
Author: Coaching for Performance

WHAT IS SECURE BASE COACHING ?

Secure Base Coaching involves caring, daring and sharing with others whether individuals, teams and organizations. The biggest challenge for coaches and those working with these concepts is the 'AND.' It is about showing an interest in others and then stretching them outside of their comfort zones in order to achieve more than they may have thought possible. This takes courage – to first connect and then to challenge and share reflections and observations for continuous improvement.

Secure Base Coaches work from the premise that each person is the expert of themselves. Therefore, they are not 'rescuing' or 'saving'' the coachee or 'telling' them what to do. Instead, they are working together to support the exploration of the coachee's thoughts, feelings, and behaviours to identify areas for growth and development. This collaborative, sharing approach encourages coachees to take ownership of their own learning and development journey, fostering a deeper sense of self-awareness and empowerment. By balancing care with challenge, Secure Base Coaches help individuals, teams and organizations to build resilience, enhance performance, and achieve their fullest potential.

"Secure Base Coaching is a transformative and practical approach for coaches to apply to individuals, teams and organizations to unleash potential and co-create the conditions where we can all 'play to thrive.'"

WHAT IS SECURE BASE COACHING ?

Acceptance and Achievement

Irrespective of culture, human beings have two psychological needs: the need for acceptance and the need for achievement. We refer to them as two legs – you need both to be grounded. If you only have one, you can function but you will be far less resilient in times of adversity.
Acceptance refers to a sense of belonging and inclusion. We are a social species and we have mirror neurons in our brains that only exist to interact with each other. It is about a sense of connection: to ourselves, others and the wider universe.
Achievement relates to a sense of purpose, meaning and being successful.
Given acceptance and achievement are our two psychological needs, what might be our two greatest fears? These are the opposites of acceptance and achievement : rejection and failure. And this is why any type of change can be so challenging: at a primal level our brain operates on the fear that if I fail, I may be rejected and if I am rejected, I may be eaten.

Therefore, the two levers to work with are what is referred to as the caring and the daring. The caring is the 'being' aspect while the daring is the 'doing' aspect.

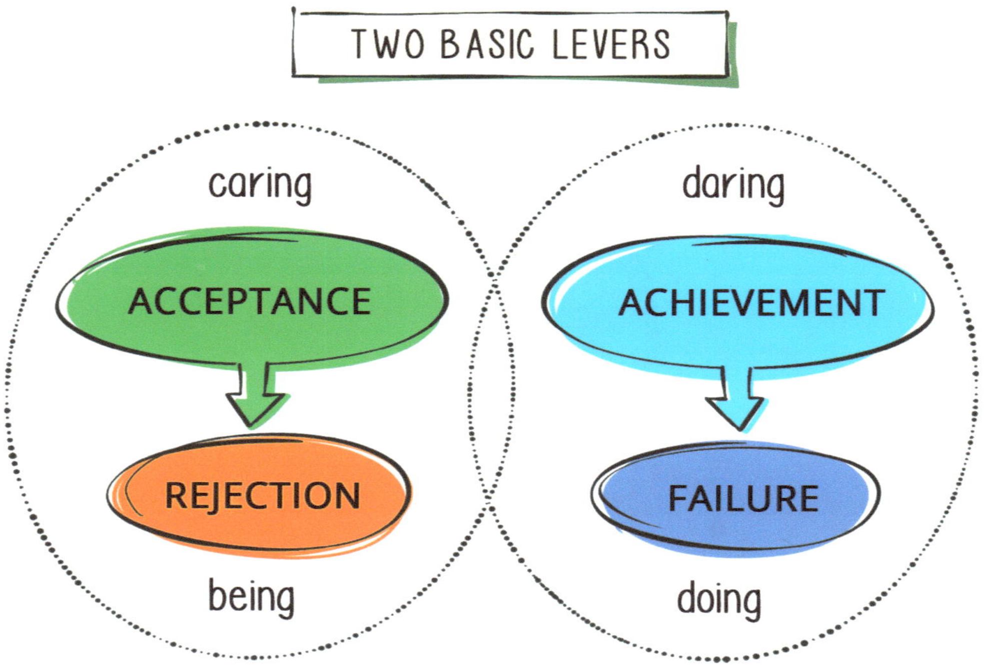

WHAT IS SECURE BASE COACHING?

The caring provides a sense of connection and interest. This builds a sense of trust. The daring is about the ability to act, giving a sense of competence: to achieve what one sets out to accomplish.
The combination of the two leads to a growing confidence in oneself and feelings of resilience, and hope in our own agency.
Sharing involves relating to those outside of self and, through dialogue around connection and competence, enhancing confidence.

It is important to stress that caring does not mean liking or friendship. It is about showing interest in others, treating them with respect, creating a connection and offering support. And the daring does not mean being aggressive or coercive. It is about challenging others to take risks, and to stretch outside comfort zones.

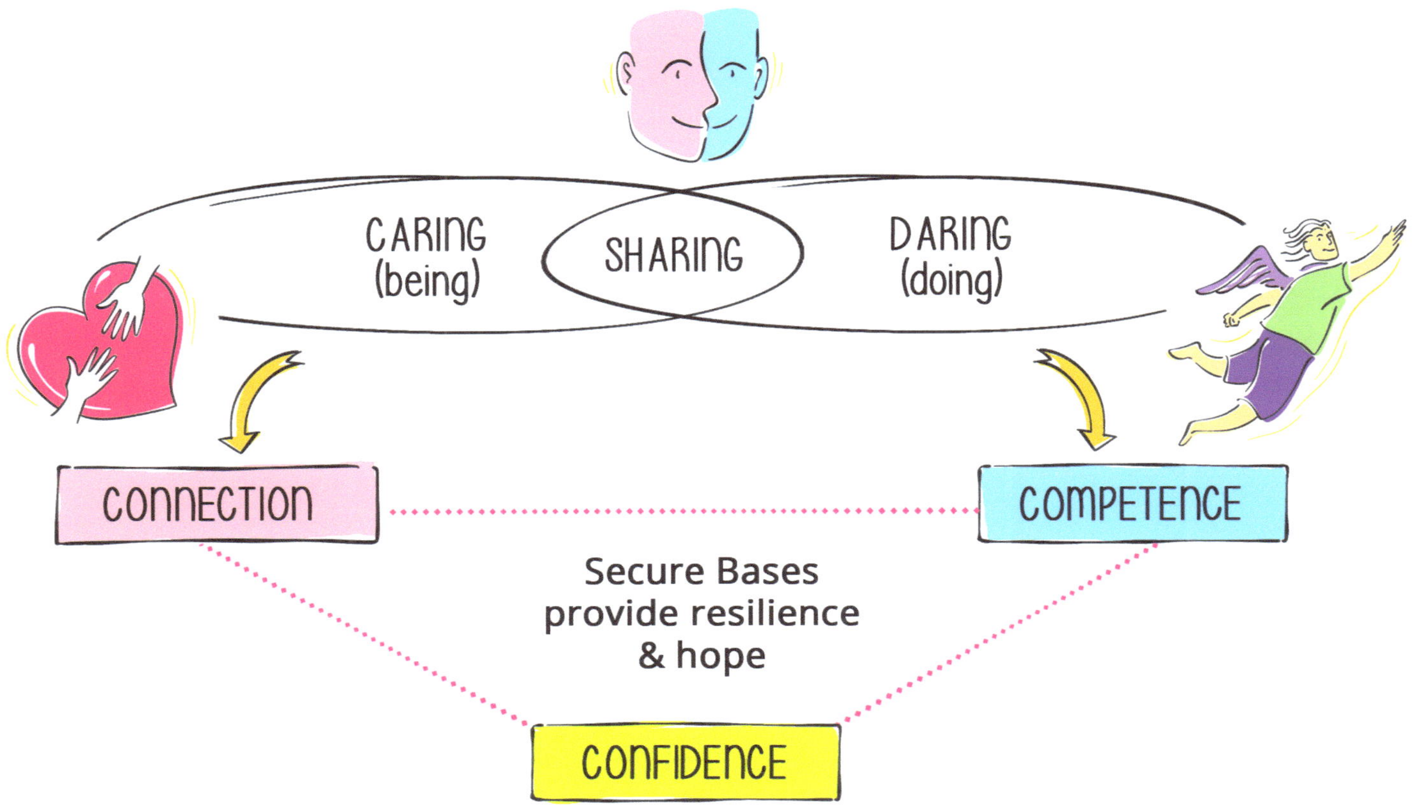

WHAT ARE SOME QUESTIONS FOR SECURE BASE COACHING ?

These questions aim to guide coaches in exploring and applying the principles of Secure Base Coaching to help individuals, teams, and organizations thrive.

Caring (Showing Interest, Respect and Acceptance)

For Individuals :

- ☑ How do you currently feel accepted and included in your team or organization ?
- ☑ What are the most meaningful relationships in your professional life, and how do they support your sense of belonging ?
- ☑ Can you share a moment when you felt genuinely cared for by a colleague or leader ? How did that impact your performance?

For Teams :

- ☑ How does your team foster a sense of inclusion and belonging among its members ?
- ☑ What practices do you have in place to ensure everyone feels heard and valued ?
- ☑ Can you identify any barriers to connection within your team, and how might you address them?

For Organizations :

- ☑ What strategies does your organization use to promote a culture of acceptance and inclusion ?
- ☑ How do you measure the effectiveness of these strategies ?
- ☑ How can leadership demonstrate care and support for employees at all levels ?

Daring (Encouraging risk-taking, Stretching outside Comfort Zones and Achievement)

For Individuals :

- ☑ What are your current professional goals, and how do they challenge you ?
- ☑ Can you recall a time when stepping out of your comfort zone led to a significant achievement ?
- ☑ How do you balance the need for acceptance with the pursuit of challenging goals ?

For Teams :

- ☑ What are the stretch goals for your team, and how do they align with individual aspirations ?
- ☑ How does your team handle failure or setbacks when pushing boundaries ?
- ☑ How do you encourage and support team members to take calculated risks ?

For Organizations :

- ☑ What initiatives are in place to foster innovation and challenge the status quo ?
- ☑ How do you support employees in taking risks and trying new approaches ?
- ☑ How do you celebrate achievements and learn from failures at an organizational level ?

WHAT ARE SOME QUESTIONS FOR SECURE BASE COACHING ?

These questions aim to guide coaches in exploring and applying the principles of Secure Base Coaching to help individuals, teams, and organizations thrive.

Sharing (Enhancing Confidence through Dialogue and Reflection)

For Individuals :

- ☑ How do you share your successes and challenges with colleagues ?
- ☑ What feedback mechanisms are in place for you to reflect on your performance ?
- ☑ How do you engage in dialogue about your growth and development with your coach or mentor ?

For Teams :

- ☑ How does your team create an environment of open and honest communication ?
- ☑ What practices do you have for sharing reflections and learning from each other's experiences ?
- ☑ How do you ensure that feedback is constructive and aimed at building confidence ?

For Organizations :

- ☑ What channels exist for employees to share their experiences and insights ?
- ☑ How do you facilitate cross-departmental or cross-functional sharing of best practices and lessons learned ?
- ☑ How does leadership model transparency and openness in sharing reflections and observations ?

Balancing Acceptance AND Achievement

For Individuals :

- ☑ How do you find balance between feeling accepted and striving for achievement ?
- ☑ What support do you need to enhance both your sense of belonging and your competence ?
- ☑ How does your sense of acceptance influence your ability to achieve your goals ?

For Teams :

- ☑ How does your team support each member's need for acceptance while also pushing for high achievement ?
- ☑ What strategies do you use to balance team cohesion with individual performance goals ?
- ☑ How do you create a culture where acceptance and achievement are seen as complementary rather than conflicting ?

For Organizations :

- ☑ How does your organizational culture support both acceptance and achievement among employees ?
- ☑ What policies or practices are in place to ensure that employees feel both valued and challenged ?
- ☑ How do you measure the balance between acceptance and achievement, and what improvements can be made ?

HOW DOES SECURE BASE COACHING CONTRIBUTE TO A GROWTH MINDSHIFT ?

Einstein is quoted as saying that the most important question that anyone can ask on a daily basis is whether the universe is hostile or whether it is friendly. It is both, but depending how you answer the question, it influences how you show up in the world.
Most people are aware of the work of Carol Dweck which looked at fixed and growth mindsets. People often ask, "Do you have a fixed mindset or a growth mindset?" Actually, that's a fixed mindset question. It is important to remember that we are ALL fixed mindset by nature (the number one job of our brain is to keep us alive and so it naturally judges), and by nurture (our societal conditioning tends to make judgments around polarities: right/wrong, good/bad, win/lose, pass/fail). Every day we have a choice: whether to operate from our default, fear-based, fixed mindset or to intervene in our habitual patterns and operate from a place of love, of opportunity and possibility by choosing a growth mindshift. The word 'mindshift' reflects the notion that our inner growth is an ongoing, never-ending journey with no 'set' end outcome.

the most fundamental question to ask every day

WHAT ARE SOME SECURE BASE COACHING QUESTIONS FOR A GROWTH MINDSHIFT ?

These questions encourage both deep reflection and active steps towards embracing a growth mindshift, aligned with the daily choice of viewing the universe as friendly and choosing to operate from a place of opportunity and possibility.

1. Reflection on Perspective:
   - How do you perceive the universe today — as a hostile place or a friendly one? How does this perception influence your daily actions and mindset?
   - Can you think of a recent situation where your view of the universe (hostile or friendly) influenced your response or decision?
2. Mindset Awareness:
   - How do you typically identify your mindset in challenging situations — do you lean towards a fixed mindset or a growth mindshift?
   - Can you identify a moment when you operated from a fixed mindset? What was the outcome, and how might it have differed with a growth mindshift approach?
3. Mindset Shift:
   - What steps can you take to shift from a fixed mindset to a growth mindshift in your daily life?
   - How can you create opportunities for yourself to practice a growth mindshift, especially in areas where you feel challenged or fearful?
4. Daily Choices:
   - What daily practices or reminders could help you choose a love, opportunity, and possibility-based response over a fear-based response?
   - How do you remind yourself of the choice you have each day to operate from a growth mindshift?
5. Impact of Mindset:
   - How has your mindset, whether fixed or growth, impacted your achievements and personal growth so far?
   - In what areas of your life would you most like to see the impact of a growth mindshift, and what first steps can you take to begin this shift?

HOW DO I COACH OTHERS TO MANAGE STATE?

Supporting the coachee in guiding their mind towards agency is an everyday challenge that requires daily practice. This is because our brains are wired at the most basic level to focus on danger and threat as a survival mechanism. Thoughts are magnetic; the more we focus on the perceived negative, the worse we feel. Conversely, when we acknowledge the pain and accept the brutal beauty of being, and then choose to focus on opportunities or possibilities, we feel healthier and more empowered. This concept aligns with the idea of "No Mud, No Lotus," which suggests that suffering and challenges (the mud) are necessary for growth and beauty (the lotus) to emerge.

By helping coachees to manage their state, coaches enable them to remain calm, focused, and effective in their interactions, thereby enhancing their ability to lead and inspire others. Through this approach, coachees can build the resilience and clarity needed to navigate complex situations and foster productive relationships.

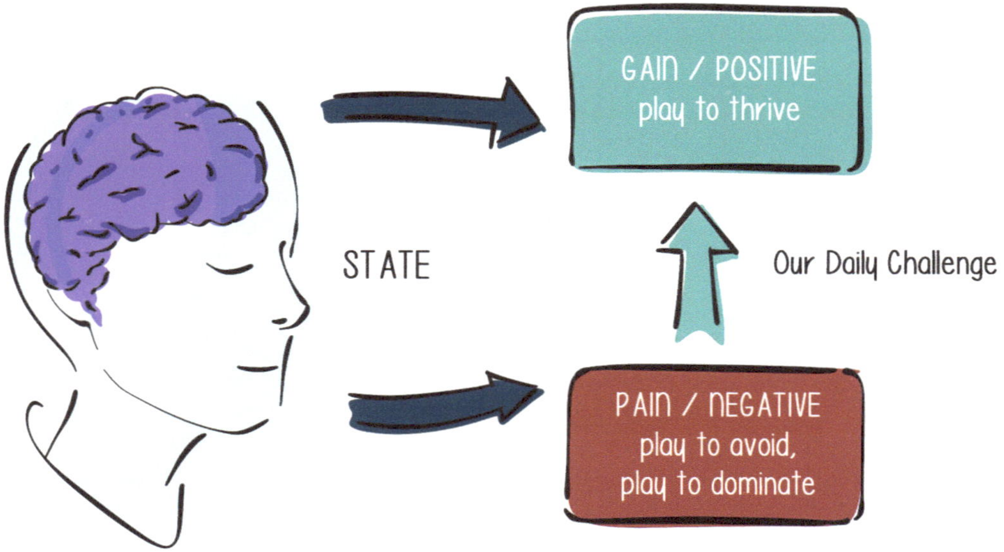

WHAT ARE SOME COACHING QUESTIONS FOR MANAGING STATE?

INDIVIDUAL LEVEL

1. ### Understanding Current State:
   - How do you currently manage your state when faced with stress or challenges?
   - Can you identify moments when you tend to focus on the negative? How does this affect your mood and actions?

2. ### Acknowledging and Accepting Pain:
   - How do you acknowledge and process feelings of pain, loss, or frustration?
   - Can you describe a situation where accepting the "brutal beauty of being" helped you find meaning or growth?

3. ### Shifting Focus to Opportunities:
   - What techniques do you use to shift your focus from negative thoughts to opportunities or possibilities?
   - Can you share an example of a time when focusing on the positive or potential outcomes improved your state and performance?

4. ### Daily Practice for Agency:
   - What daily practices or routines help you guide your mind towards a sense of agency and empowerment?
   - How do you remind yourself to practice these techniques regularly to rewire your brain towards seeing the glass as 'half-full'?

5. ### Embracing "No Mud, No Lotus":
   - How do you perceive the concept of "No Mud, No Lotus" in your personal and professional life?
   - Can you think of a recent challenge (the mud) that led to significant growth or a positive outcome (the lotus)?

WHAT ARE SOME COACHING QUESTIONS FOR MANAGING STATE?

TEAM LEVEL

Collective State Management:

1.
- How does your team support each other in managing stress and maintaining a positive state?
- What strategies can your team implement to collectively acknowledge and process 'challenging' emotions?

Encouraging Positive Focus:

2.
- How can your team encourage a culture of focusing on opportunities and possibilities, especially during tough times?
- What practices can your team adopt to reinforce the habit of looking for the silver lining in challenging situations?

Daily Practices for Team Agency:

3.
- What daily or regular practices can your team engage in to foster a sense of agency and empowerment among its members?
- How can your team hold each other accountable for maintaining these practices?

Embracing "no Mud, no Lotus":

4.
- How does your team embrace and process emotions like loss, grief, sadness, and panic during the change curve to foster growth and resilience?

WHAT ARE SOME COACHING QUESTIONS FOR MANAGING STATE?

ORGANIZATIONAL LEVEL

1
Organizational Support for State Management:

- How does your organization support employees in managing their state and maintaining focus and calm under pressure?
- What programs or resources are available to help employees acknowledge and process 'challenging' emotions effectively?

2
Promoting a Positive Organizational Focus:

- How does your organization promote a culture of focusing on opportunities and possibilities?
- What initiatives can be introduced to encourage employees to view challenges as opportunities for growth?

3
Institutionalizing Daily Practices:

- What daily practices can the organization encourage to help employees feel empowered and maintain a positive state?
- How can the organization integrate the concept of "No Mud, No Lotus" into its values and culture to support resilience and growth?

4
Creating Secure Base Spaces:

- How can your organization create and sustain secure base spaces that foster psychological safety, allowing employees to express vulnerability, and share and celebrate successes and failures?

HOW DO I COACH OTHERS TO CREATE CONNECTIONS ?

It is important to remember that we are a social species and that we have mirror neurons in our brains that only exist to interact with each other. Research indicates that our basic need for connection, empathy and bonding is actually a biological wiring that is activated through a learning process that involves watching others and experiencing how they relate.

The Bonding Cycle has four stages: Attachment, Bonding, Separation and Grief. We are all operating across the whole Bonding Cycle on a daily basis as it is a core part of the complexity of being human.

Attachment is about proximity and feeling a sense of comfort so that we can let down our guard. Attachments have the potential to become emotional bonds where an exchange of energy or interest occurs. All bonds eventually lead to separation which is a disruption of the bonding and leads to a preparation for grief which prompts a change in identity. Grief involves saying goodbye in order to say hello. It is about working through the loss to come back to the joy of living.

THE BONDING CYCLE

ref : Kohlrieser

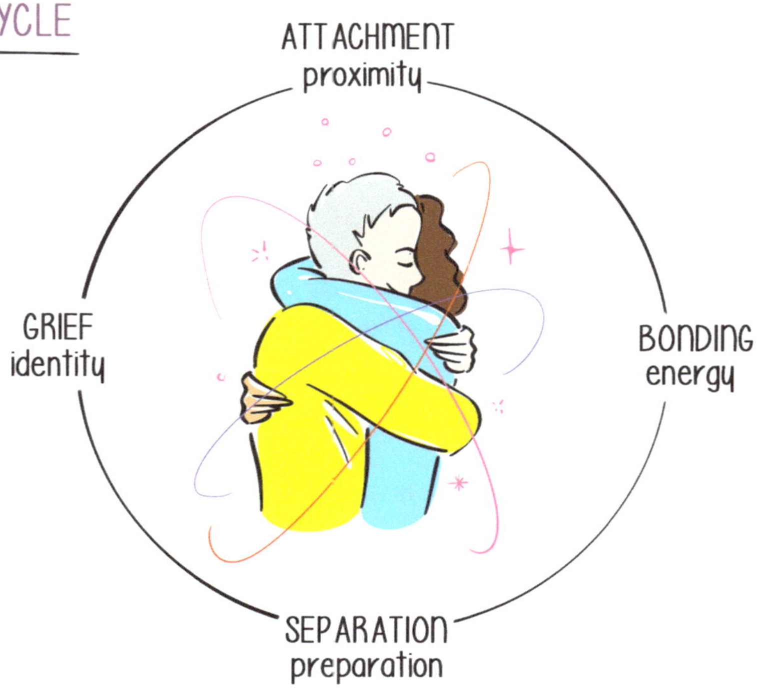

WHAT ARE SOME COACHING QUESTIONS FOR CREATING CONNECTIONS ?

INDIVIDUAL LEVEL

1. Understanding Attachment:
   - How do you typically form attachments with others in your personal and professional life ?
   - Can you describe a situation where feeling a sense of comfort and attachment allowed you to let down your guard ?

2. Exploring Bonding:
   - How do you differentiate between simple attachment and deeper emotional bonds ?
   - Can you share an example of a relationship where an attachment evolved into a strong emotional bond ? What factors contributed to this deepening of the connection ?

3. Navigating Separation:
   - How do you typically handle separations in your relationships, both personal and professional ?
   - Can you recall a time when a separation disrupted a bond? How did you prepare for and manage the resulting emotions ?

4. Processing Grief:
   - How do you process grief and loss in your relationships ?
   - Can you think of an instance where working through grief helped you find new joy or growth? How did this process unfold for you ?

WHAT ARE SOME COACHING QUESTIONS FOR CREATING CONNECTIONS?

TEAM LEVEL

1 Facilitating Attachment in Teams:

- How does your team create an environment that fosters attachment and a sense of comfort among its members?
- What practices can your team implement to strengthen initial attachments into deeper bonds?

2 Building Bonds within the Team:

- How does your team ensure that bonds are nurtured and maintained over time?
- Can you share an example of a team project or activity that significantly strengthened the bonds between team members?

3 Managing Separation in Teams:

- How does your team handle separations, such as members leaving or projects ending?
- What strategies can your team use to prepare for and manage the emotional impact of these separations?

4 Supporting Grief and Transition:

- How does your team support members who are experiencing grief or loss, whether personal or professional?
- What initiatives can your team take to help members transition from grief back to a sense of joy and engagement?

WHAT ARE SOME COACHING QUESTIONS FOR CREATING CONNECTIONS?

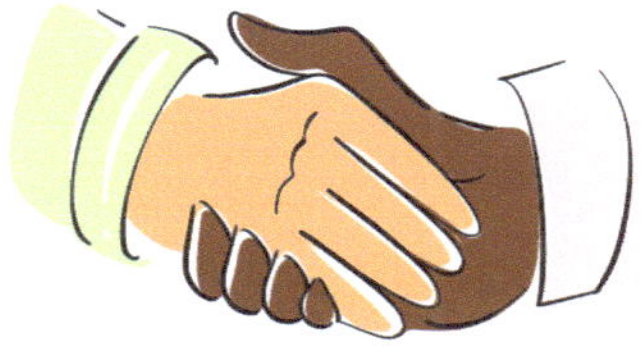

ORGANIZATIONAL LEVEL

1. **Promoting Attachment Organizationally:**
   - How does your organization create a culture that supports the formation of attachments among employees?
   - What policies or practices can be introduced to foster a sense of comfort and security within the organization?

2. **Enhancing Organizational Bonding:**
   - How does your organization facilitate the development of strong bonds between employees and teams?
   - Can you provide examples of programs or activities that have successfully strengthened organizational bonds?

3. **Addressing Separation Organizationally:**
   - How does your organization manage the process of separations, such as employee turnover or departmental changes?
   - What measures can your organization take to support employees through these transitions and minimize disruption?

4. **Navigating Organizational Grief:**
   - How does your organization support employees in processing grief and loss, whether due to personal or organizational changes?
   - What resources or programs can be implemented to help employees navigate grief and return to a sense of purpose and joy?

HOW DO I COACH OTHERS TO EXPLORE THEIR SECURE BASES?

In the book Care to Dare, secure bases are defined as:

"a person, place, goal or object that provides a sense of protection, safety and caring and offers a source of inspiration and energy for daring, exploration, risk-taking and seeking challenge."

Secure bases shut down the fear response in the brain and provide the energy and inspiration to seek out new challenges. The more secure bases you have, the better. And it is never too late to find secure bases or learn to become a secure base for others. Secure bases shape our beliefs about ourselves which then influences the way we are in the world and the confidence that we have to take risks.
Any entity that, through interaction, enhances a person's inner sense of acceptance and inspires exploration can be a form of secure base. Whilst secure bases can be places, events, experiences, beliefs, goals and even symbols, the most powerful are undoubtedly people. Someone who is deceased can remain a secure base for a person when experiences with them, the impact they had and the beliefs formed from the relationship are internalized.

HOW DO I COACH OTHERS TO EXPLORE THEIR SECURE BASES?

You can use a chart like the one below to ask people to reflect upon and write in the secure bases in their life.

PEOPLE	PLACES
EVENTS	EXPERIENCES
BELIEFS	GOALS
SYMBOLS	OTHER

WHAT ARE SOME COACHING QUESTIONS FOR EXPLORING SECURE BASES ?

Rather than advocating a position, a secure base coach applies the judicious use of questions to challenge the coachee. These questions are designed to help you explore the concept of secure bases, understand their importance, and reflect on their impact on your life and others.

1. Definition Clarification:
   - How do you understand the concept of a "secure base" as defined in "Care to Dare"?
   - What elements of this definition resonate with you most?

2. Personal Identification:
   - Who or what in your life acts as a secure base for you?
   - How do these secure bases provide you with a sense of protection and inspiration?

3. People as Secure Bases:
   - Can you identify a person in your life who has been a significant secure base for you? How have they influenced you?
   - What qualities do you think make someone an effective secure base?

4. Other Secure Bases:
   - Aside from people, what places, goals, or objects serve as secure bases for you?
   - How do these secure bases contribute to your sense of safety and motivation?

5. Turning Off the 'Flashlight of Fear':
   - Can you recall a time when a secure base helped you turn off your 'flashlight of fear' and enabled you to take risks or face challenges?
   - How did this impact your resilience and ability to focus?

WHAT ARE SOME COACHING QUESTIONS FOR EXPLORING SECURE BASES?

6 Challenges and Exploration:

- In what ways have your secure bases encouraged you to take on new challenges and explore new opportunities?
- How do these experiences shape your personal and professional growth?

7 Strengthening Secure Bases:

- What steps can you take to strengthen your existing secure bases or identify new ones?
- How can you cultivate relationships or environments that provide a stronger sense of security and inspiration?

8 Supporting Others:

- How can you be a secure base for others in your personal or professional life?
- What actions can you take to ensure you provide a sense of protection and inspiration for those around you?

9 Integrating into Daily Life:

- How can you integrate the concept of secure bases into your daily life to enhance your resilience and focus?
- What small changes can you make to ensure your secure bases are accessible and supportive when needed?

10 Continuous Reflection:

- How often do you reflect on your secure bases and their impact on your life?
- What methods can you use to regularly assess and appreciate the secure bases in your life?

WHY IS PLAYING TO THRIVE SO VITAL ?

From our research for the book Care to Dare, we looked at what made leaders, teams and organizations high-performing.
When people demonstrate respect, interest and support AND challenge, take risks and stretch outside comfort zones, they find themselves in the 'play to thrive' space. It takes courage to be in this quadrant as you have to connect with others and then challenge them. However, this secure base approach releases productive energy and it is where creativity, curiosity and innovation flourish. It is a 'power-with' approach where people co-create the conditions where they can thrive in a healthy and sustainable manner. Being in this secure base space also contributes to psychological health and wellbeing.

Now, no-one spends all of their time in the 'play to thrive' quadrant. It is important to have some 'rest and recovery' where people step off the challenge whilst keeping the connection. However, if they spend too long in the 'play not to lose' space they can become complacent. It is a comfortable energy and can feel like a cocoon. Similarly, when people focus too much on the dare and not enough on the care, they can move into the 'Play to Dominate' space. This is often driven by a fear-based response to stress or external pressures and leads to micromanagement and the illusion of control. This releases a corrosive energy where people do not feel trusted and there is little psychological safety. If a leader is too much in 'play to dominate' then others can move into 'play to avoid,' a resigned energy where they withdraw engagement and do the minimum.

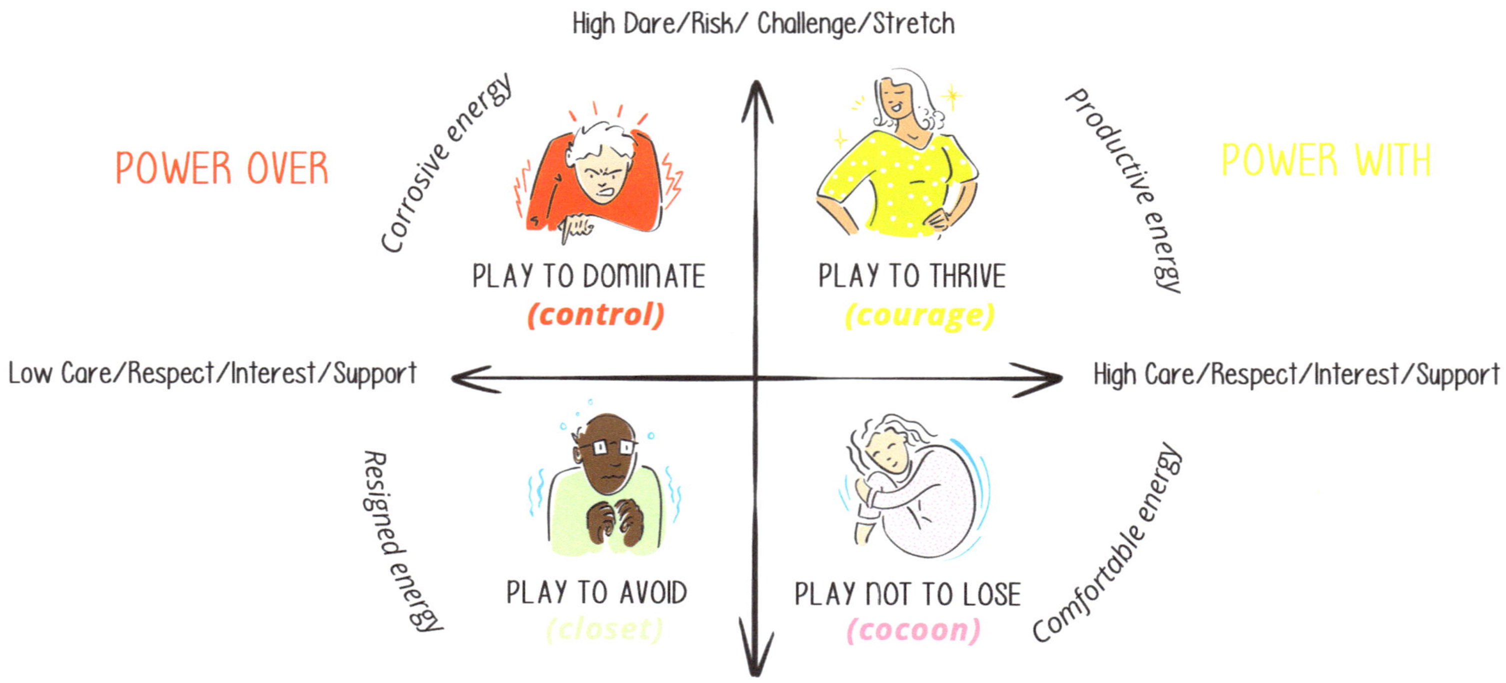

HOW DO I COACH THE QUADRANTS ?

These questions aim to foster reflection, growth, and action at individual, team and organizational levels, encouraging a shift towards healthy & sustainable high performance, innovation, and well-being.

INDIVIDUAL LEVEL

1 Self-Reflection and Growth:

- How often do you find yourself in the 'play to thrive' space? Can you describe a recent experience where you felt both supported and challenged?
- What steps can you take to balance care and dare in your daily activities to ensure you stay in the 'play to thrive' quadrant?

2 Courage and Connection:

- Can you recall a situation where you had to connect deeply with someone and then challenge them? How did it feel, and what was the outcome?
- What are some areas in your life where you can take more risks while ensuring you have the necessary support?

3 Navigating Separation:

- How do you manage your need for 'rest and recovery' without slipping into complacency or 'play not to lose'?
- When you feel the urge to micromanage, what strategies can you use to shift towards a 'power-with' approach that fosters creativity and trust?

HOW DO I COACH THE QUADRANTS ?

These questions aim to foster reflection, growth, and action at individual, team and organizational levels, encouraging a shift towards healthy & sustainable high performance, innovation, and well-being.

TEAM LEVEL

1 Team Dynamics:

- How does your team balance respect, interest, and support with the need to challenge and take risks? Can you provide an example?
- In what ways can your team create a secure base environment that encourages everyone to thrive and innovate?

2 Courageous Collaboration:

- How can your team members better connect with each other to foster a culture of co-creation and mutual growth?
- What specific actions can your team take to move from 'play not to lose' or 'play to dominate' towards 'play to thrive'?

3 Team Well-being:

- How does your team ensure adequate 'rest and recovery' periods to maintain high performance and avoid burnout?
- What are the signs that your team might be slipping into 'play to avoid,' and how can you collectively address this to re-engage and motivate each other?

HOW DO I COACH THE QUADRANTS ?

These questions aim to foster reflection, growth, and action at individual, team and organizational levels, encouraging a shift towards healthy & sustainable high performance, innovation, and well-being.

ORGANIZATIONAL LEVEL

1 Organizational Culture:

- How does your organization demonstrate a balance of care and dare in its leadership practices and overall culture?
- What initiatives can your organization implement to foster a 'play to thrive' environment for all employees?

2 Leadership and Innovation:

- How can your organization support leaders in developing the courage to connect deeply and challenge effectively?
- What structures or processes can be put in place to encourage innovation and creativity across the organization?

3 Sustainable Performance:

- How does your organization promote psychological health and well-being among its employees?
- What strategies can be used to identify and mitigate the risks of slipping into 'play to dominate,' 'play not to lose' or 'play to avoid' behaviors within the organization?

HOW DO I COACH THE SECURE BASE CATEGORIES AND CHARACTERISTICS ?

In our research for Care to Dare, we looked at the characteristics that high performing executives, as rated by their employees, displayed on a day-to-day basis. It is important to stress that no-one had a perfect score across all nine characteristics. In fact, the best-rated leaders were seen to be doing five or six well. Remember, none of us is perfect. Each of us is naturally talented in some of these characteristics and, where we're not, we can always practice and develop our skills. To aid in their use as a coaching tool, the nine characteristics have been placed under three key categories for cultivating a secure base approach: Conscious Choice, Constructive Challenge and Courageous Communication.

CONSCIOUS CHOICE	CONSTRUCTIVE CHALLENGE	COURAGEOUS COMMUNICATION
Stays Calm	**Sees the Potential**	**Uses Listening & Inquiry**
• Mindfulness • Four deep breaths • Keeps perpective • Leads others	• Believes in potential to develop • Growth versus fixed mindset • Stretches & challenges the individual • Statements of belief	• Uses open-ended questions • Encourages discovery • Active listening • Words/tone/body language
Accepts the Individual	**Encourages Risk-taking**	**Delivers Powerful Messages**
• Unconditional positive regard • I'm ok, you're ok • Separates the person from the problem • Collective consciousness	• Confidence to let go of control • Focuses self and others on stepping out of comfort zones • Creates opportunities for others to shine • Supports others to excel	• Short, sharp phrases • Four sentence rule • Repetition • Congruence
Focuses on the Positive	**Inspires through Intrinsic Motivation**	**Signals Accessibility**
• Looks for the learning • Switches from negative to positive • Sells the benefits of pain • Helps others to see the positive	• Self-driven & motivated • Instills a sense of achievement • Desire to 'make a difference' somehow • Leverages the power of the team	• Believed to be accessible • Responds to requests in a timely fashion • Mentally available • Takes time to reach out

MAKING A CONSCIOUS CHOICE

The three characteristics that fall under the Conscious Choice category are Stays Calm, Accepts the Individual and Focuses on the Positive.

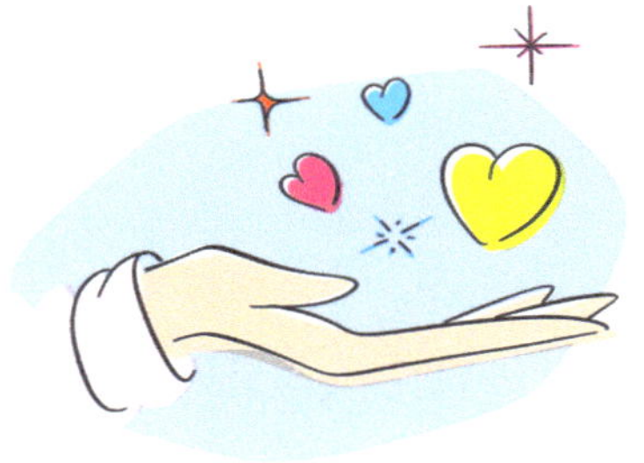

From a coaching perspective, human beings possess the remarkable agency to make conscious choices, enabling them to intervene in habitual and conditioned patterns that may limit their potential. By staying calm, being mindful, and utilizing breathwork, individuals can create a state of mental clarity and emotional regulation, as supported by neuroscience research on the benefits of mindfulness and breathing techniques in reducing stress and enhancing cognitive function. Accepting the individual with unconditional positive regard, while focusing on the positive and acknowledging the negative, fosters a supportive environment where growth and resilience can flourish. This practice is rooted in the understanding that the brain's neural pathways can be rewired through consistent daily practices, such as mindfulness, gratitude and positive thinking, to see the glass as 'half-full.' Neuroplasticity, the brain's ability to reorganize itself by forming new neural connections, underscores the importance of these intentional practices in transforming one's mindset and behaviors over time. By embracing these strategies, coaches can work with coachees to cultivate a more optimistic and proactive approach to life's challenges, ultimately leading to greater well-being and success.

CONSCIOUS CHOICE

Stays Calm

- Mindfulness
- Four deep breaths
- Keeps perpective
- Leads others

Accepts the Individual

- Unconditional positive regard
- I'm ok, you're ok
- Separates the person from the problem
- Collective consciousness

Focuses on the Positive

- Looks for the learning
- Switches from negative to positive
- Sells the benefits of pain
- Helps others to see the positive

Stays Calm

In our research, this was the most frequently quoted characteristic and, given the uncertainty in today's world, it is so important to find ways to manage yours and others' anxiety. The number one function of our brain is to keep us alive, and so it is constantly looking for potential threats. Therefore, in times of stress, people need to be reassured that they're not in danger and that others can handle the situation, whatever it might be. By combining direction and clarity while staying compassionate and connected to people, feelings of well-being and trust are enhanced. Remember just like a smile or yawn, emotions are contagious. By remaining outwardly calm a person can instill confidence in those around them and reduce any sense of panic.

What can your coachee do to practice keeping calm? Here are three exercises for them to apply to cultivate the ability to stay calm:

Exercise 1:

Many of us can get caught up in the business of busyness. Step off the hamster wheel every day by taking four deep breaths through the nose. This slows your heart rate and increases oxygen in your system helping you switch states and shift your attention away from the stress.

Exercise 2:

Practice noticing your emotions and asking yourself why you are feeling a certain way. Acknowledge your moods. Notice the emotion, digest it and let it go if it is unhelpful. A simple way to do this is to write it down, then screw up the piece of paper and throw it away.

Exercise 3:

Practice mini-mindful moments: a few times per day, take 30 seconds or a minute to stop and listen to the sounds around you and change your visual focus as well: look out of a window or take a walk in fresh air.

Stays Calm: Coaching Questions

INDIVIDUAL LEVEL

1

Self-Awareness:

- What are some signs that indicate you are starting to feel stressed? How do you typically respond to these signs?
- Can you describe a situation where you remained calm under stress? What strategies did you use?

2

Stress Management Techniques:

- What techniques or practices help you stay calm when faced with stressful situations?
- How can you incorporate more of these techniques into your daily routine to better manage stress?

3

Reflection and Learning:

- Reflect on a recent stressful event where you felt overwhelmed. What could you have done differently to stay calm?
- How do you usually debrief after a stressful situation to learn and improve your response for the future?

4

Building Resilience:

- How do you build and maintain resilience to better handle future stressful situations?
- What specific actions or habits contribute to your ability to stay calm under pressure?

Stays Calm: Coaching Questions

TEAM LEVEL

Team Dynamics:

1

- How does your team typically respond to stressful situations? Are there members who serve as calming influences?
- What practices can your team implement to support each other in staying calm during high-pressure times?

Collective Stress Management:

2

- What stress management techniques can your team adopt collectively to maintain composure under pressure?
- How can your team create an environment that minimizes unnecessary stress and promotes calmness?

Support Systems:

3

- How does your team ensure that support is available for members who are struggling with stress?
- What can your team do to recognize and address stress early before it escalates?

Building Resilience:

4

- How can your team build collective resilience to better handle future stressful situations?
- What specific actions or strategies will your team implement to enhance its ability to stay calm under pressure?

Stays Calm: Coaching Questions

ORGANIZATIONAL LEVEL

Organizational Culture:

1

- How does your organization promote a culture of calm and resilience in the face of stress?
- What policies or practices are in place to help employees manage stress effectively?

Training and Resources:

2

- What training programs or resources does your organization offer to help employees stay calm under stress?
- How can the organization improve these offerings to better support employees?

Leadership Example:

3

- How do leaders in your organization model staying calm under stress? Can you share an example of effective leadership in a stressful situation?
- What steps can leaders take to ensure they are setting a positive example for stress management?

Employee Support and Well-being:

4

- How does your organization ensure continuous support for employee well-being and stress management?
- What additional initiatives can be introduced to foster a supportive and calm work environment?

Accepts the Individual

This characteristic is about separating the person from the problem, applying an 'I'm Ok, You're OK' philosophy and being aware of collective consciousness. Acceptance of my counterpart with all their diverse characteristics is the basic prerequisite for an inclusive approach to each other. This attitude also has a positive influence on the entire environment. Of course, accepting the individual can be quite challenging and the more you practice, the better you become.

A willingness to forgive may seem like a superhuman feat but, at the end of the day, we are a social species and acceptance is fundamental to our survival. It is also vital in turning off our focus on fear. When we don't feel accepted, we are less open to being challenged or stretched. Core to this is the Rogerian concept of unconditional positive regard – that everyone deserves to be the recipient of a basic human respect. This characteristic also has relevance for inclusion and diversity. It is vital to embrace difference. A mindset of acceptance expands our horizons to respect other humans as well as the other species with whom we share this planet.

How can your coachee practice accepting the individual? Here are three exercises they can work on for this characteristic:

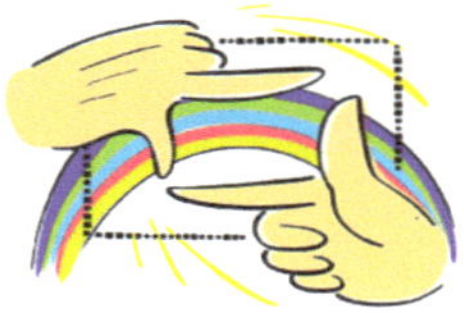

Exercise 1:

Practice getting into a state of unconditional positive regard at least once per day. Reflect on the interconnectivity of all living things and, amongst the suffering, look for the goodness in people and life

Exercise 2:

Notice and let go of any instant judgments, whether from your own inner critic towards yourself or whether towards others

Exercise 3:

Separate the person from the problem by asking yourself under what circumstances would a reasonable person act this way?

Accepts the Individual: Coaching Questions

INDIVIDUAL LEVEL

1 Self-Reflection:

- Can you recall a time when you successfully separated a person's behavior from their intrinsic value as an individual? What was the outcome?
- How do you remind yourself to maintain an "I'm OK, you're OK" attitude during challenging interactions?

2 Application of Unconditional Positive Regard:

- How do you practice unconditional positive regard in your personal and professional relationships?
- What challenges do you face when trying to apply unconditional positive regard, and how do you overcome them?

3 Empathy and Understanding:

- How do you ensure that you are truly understanding and accepting of the person, even when you disagree with their actions or perspectives?
- What strategies do you use to stay empathetic and non-judgmental in difficult situations?

4 Promoting Inclusivity:

- How can you actively promote and embrace diversity in your interactions and relationships?
- What specific actions will you take to enhance inclusivity in your environment?

Accepts the Individual: Coaching Questions

TEAM LEVEL

Team Dynamics:

1
- How does your team practice acceptance and unconditional positive regard among its members?
- Can you think of a recent team conflict where separating the person from the problem helped in resolving the issue?

Building a Supportive Environment:

2
- What steps can your team take to ensure that all members feel accepted and valued, regardless of their mistakes or differing opinions?
- How can your team foster an environment where the "I'm OK, you're OK" attitude is the norm?

Conflict Resolution:

3
- How does your team handle conflicts in a way that maintains respect for each individual while addressing the problem at hand?
- What processes or practices can your team implement to better separate personal judgments from professional critiques?

Promoting Inclusivity:

4
- How can your team actively promote and embrace diversity within the team?
- What specific actions will your team take to enhance inclusivity and respect for differences?

Accepts the Individual: Coaching Questions

ORGANIZATIONAL LEVEL

Organizational Culture:

1
- How does your organization promote the principles of unconditional positive regard and acceptance of individuals?
- What initiatives or programs are in place to encourage an "I'm OK, you're OK" attitude throughout the organization?

Leadership and Modeling:

2
- How do leaders in your organization demonstrate acceptance and unconditional positive regard in their interactions?
- What examples can you share of leaders effectively separating the person from the problem?

Policy and Practice:

3
- What policies or practices can your organization adopt to better support the acceptance of individuals while addressing performance or behavioral issues?
- How can the organization create a culture where feedback is given in a way that separates the person from the problem and maintains mutual respect?

Inclusion and Diversity:

4
- How does your organization actively promote and embrace inclusion at all levels?
- What specific actions or programs are in place to ensure a culture of respect and acceptance for all employees?

Focuses on the Positive

When confronted with challenges, each experience is also an invitation to learn. There is an expression that every cloud has a silver lining. It is important to acknowledge the pain and then to reflect on the opportunities or possibilities. This involves looking for learning, switching from a negative state to a positive one, 'selling' the benefits of pain and helping others to also see a positive, an opportunity or a possibility. It is about naming the sharks and then focusing on the dolphins. Secure base coaches encourage coachees to first acknowledge pain or loss and then gradually reframe to the benefit or opportunity. They create a sense of hope, both in the present and in the future, that unleashes a dynamic energy with forward momentum. Research studies indicate that a sense of hope is vital for human flourishing and wellbeing. And hope is also a contagious emotion. A strong purpose, goal or vision is an important aspect in providing meaning and helps people to focus their minds on possibility.

What can you do to develop your coachee's capacity to focus on the positive? Ask your coachee to try out these three exercises:

Exercise 1:
Pick three people and focus on a positive in your interactions, sharing with them what you appreciated.

Exercise 2:
Practice reframing something that you didn't like during the day by looking for the benefit in the pain or for the learning you gained.

Exercise 3:
Before sleep, focus on two or three things that you are grateful for that day.

MAKING A CONSCIOUS CHOICE

Focuses on the Positive: Coaching Questions

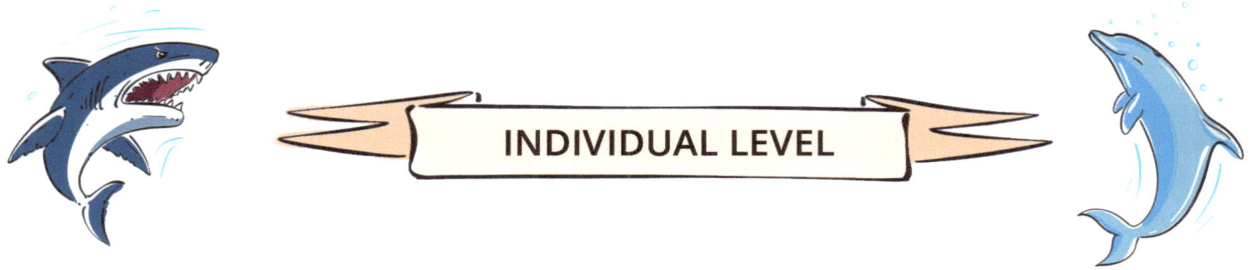

Acknowledging Pain and Grief:

1

- Can you describe a recent situation where you experienced pain or grief? How did you acknowledge and process these emotions?
- What strategies do you use to allow yourself to fully experience and understand your feelings of pain and grief?

Finding the Learning:

2

- After acknowledging your pain, what lessons or insights have you gained from the experience?
- How can you apply these learnings to future situations to improve your resilience and response?

Seeing the Positive:

3

- Can you think of a challenging situation where you were able to find a positive aspect or opportunity? What was it?
- What helps you shift your focus from the negative aspects to the potential positives in a situation?

Setting Intentions:

4

- How can setting a daily goal or intention that brings you joy or fulfillment influence your overall mindset and actions?
- What goal will you set for yourself tomorrow?

MAKING A CONSCIOUS CHOICE

Focuses on the Positive: Coaching Questions

TEAM LEVEL

1 Team Acknowledgment of Challenges:

- How does your team collectively acknowledge and address pain and grief when faced with difficult situations?
- What practices can your team implement to ensure everyone feels heard and supported during tough times?

2 Learning Together:

- How does your team reflect on challenging experiences to identify lessons and opportunities for growth?
- Can you share an example of a time when your team turned a negative situation into a learning opportunity?

3 Cultivating a Positive Outlook:

- How does your team encourage each other to see the silver lining or potential opportunities in difficult circumstances?
- What steps can your team take to build a culture that focuses on positive outcomes and continuous learning?

4 Setting Collective Goals:

- How can your team set collective goals or intentions that foster a sense of unity and positivity?
- What is a specific goal your team can work towards together?

Focuses on the Positive: Coaching Questions

Organizational Approach to Pain and Grief:

1

- How does your organization acknowledge and support employees through periods of pain and grief?
- What initiatives are in place to help employees process and cope with difficult experiences?

Organizational Learning:

2

- How does your organization use challenging situations as opportunities for learning and improvement?
- Can you share an example of a significant challenge the organization faced and the positive outcomes that resulted from it?

Promoting a Positive Culture:

3

- What policies or practices does your organization have to promote a focus on positive outcomes and opportunities in every situation?
- How can the organization better support leaders and employees in finding the silver lining in challenging times?

Fostering Collective Resilience:

4

- How does your organization foster collective resilience and adaptability in the face of ongoing challenges?
- What specific strategies can be implemented to strengthen this resilience?

PROVIDING CONSTRUCTIVE CHALLENGE

The three characteristics that fall under the Constructive Challenge category are Sees the Potential, Encourages Risk-taking and Inspires through Intrinsic Motivation.

From a coaching perspective, providing constructive challenge is essential to assist a coachee in stepping outside their comfort zones and realizing their full potential. By seeing the potential in themselves and others, coaches can encourage risk-taking and inspire through intrinsic motivation, fostering a belief in the coachee's capabilities. Just as in sports coaching, where athletes are pushed to their limits to achieve peak performance, the process of being challenged is crucial for personal and professional growth. This approach requires the coach to possess an inner confidence and remain grounded in the relationship with the coachee, ensuring that challenges are presented in the coachee's best interests. By creating a supportive yet challenging environment, coaches help coachees embrace discomfort as a pathway to growth, develop resilience, and build the courage to take risks. This dynamic not only promotes significant achievements but also instills a lasting sense of empowerment and self-efficacy.

CONSTRUCTIVE CHALLENGE
Sees the Potential
• Believes in potential to develop • Growth versus fixed mindset • Stretches & challenges the individual • Statements of belief
Encourages Risk-taking
• Confidence to let go of control • Focuses self and others on stepping out of comfort zones • Creates opportunities for others to shine • Supports others to excel
Inspires through Intrinsic Motivation
• Self-driven & motivated • Instills a sense of achievement • Desire to 'make a difference' somehow • Leverages the power of the team

Sees the Potential

By recognizing and acknowledging potential, either in yourself or in others, an environment can be created that opens up possibilities and opportunities. This characteristic is an important aspect of unleashing the potential of every individual.
Secure Base coaches believe that every person can learn, grow or improve even if this is only by a small amount.
They view the living world as one full of opportunity and their role in it is to create the conditions where people can fulfil their potential.
Here are three exercises your coachee can practice:

Exercise 1:

Notice when you are using a fixed mindset (black and white thinking) versus a growth mindshift of possibility

Exercise 2:

Think about every person you interact with this week and the potential they have to improve

Exercise 3:

Work on coachable moments: take the opportunity to ask questions or give feedback to support the growth of others

Sees the Potential: Coaching Questions

1 Believing in Potential:

- Can you share an instance where you recognized untapped potential in yourself? How did you work towards developing it?
- How do you maintain belief in your potential, especially when faced with setbacks or challenges?

2 Applying a Growth Mindshift:

- What does having a growth mindset mean to you, and how do you apply it in your daily life?
- How do you move from a fixed mindset to a growth mindshift when encountering a difficult situation?

3 Stretching and Challenging Yourself:

- What are some recent goals or challenges you've set for yourself to stretch beyond your comfort zone?
- How do you ensure that these challenges are both achievable and growth-oriented?

4 Using Belief Statements:

- What positive belief statements do you use to motivate and encourage yourself?
- Can you identify a belief statement that has helped you overcome a significant obstacle?

PROVIDING CONSTRUCTIVE CHALLENGE

Sees the Potential: Coaching Questions

TEAM LEVEL

1 Believing in Team Potential:

- How do you identify and nurture the potential in your team members?
- What strategies do you use to communicate your belief in their abilities and potential?

2 Fostering a Growth Mindshift in the Team:

- How does your team cultivate a growth mindshift culture where learning and development are prioritized?
- What practices can your team adopt to encourage each other to embrace challenges and view failures as learning opportunities?

3 Stretching and Challenging the Team:

- What are some recent challenges your team has undertaken to push beyond its current capabilities?
- How does your team support each other in achieving these stretch goals?

4 Using Belief Statements in the Team:

- What belief statements or affirmations does your team use to foster a positive and motivating environment?
- How can your team incorporate more belief statements into daily interactions to reinforce a culture of potential and growth?

PROVIDING CONSTRUCTIVE CHALLENGE

Sees the Potential: Coaching Questions

ORGANIZATIONAL LEVEL

1. **Believing in Organizational Potential**
   - How does your organization identify and develop the potential within its workforce?
   - What initiatives are in place to ensure that employees feel valued and believed in?

2. **Cultivating a Growth Mindshift in the Organization:**
   - How does your organization promote a growth mindshift among employees at all levels?
   - What training or development programs are available to help employees adopt and maintain a growth mindshift?

3. **Stretching and Challenging the Organization:**
   - What ambitious goals has your organization set to drive growth and innovation?
   - How does the organization support employees in meeting these challenges and stretching their capabilities?

4. **Using Belief Statements Organizationally:**
   - How does your organization use belief statements to inspire and motivate employees?
   - What steps can the organization take to integrate belief statements into its culture and communication strategies?

Encourages Risk-taking

This characteristic could be misunderstood at first. The point here is not to promote taking reckless or ill-advised risks. Rather, this characteristic is about moving yourself and others outside of comfort zones. Creativity and Innovation occur when we challenge ourselves to think beyond the status quo. By actively involving employees and creating a sense of 'psychological safety' you can encourage them to think 'outside the box' and consider new ideas and innovative ways of working that could be of enormous benefit in this changing world. By taking risks, learning and adapting, people are able to fulfil their potential.

When a child learns to ride a bike, you may hold the back of the saddle but if you never let go, they never learn to ride. When you first let go, they may wobble or fall, and that is when you encourage them to keep trying.
A number of organizations I know use "Get out of jail free" (GOOJF) cards to build psychological safety and to create an environment where it is OK to share failures. The idea is that at the monthly meeting, there is a standing agenda item entitled Get Out of Jail Free. Any member of the team can then 'play their card' sharing a mistake they have made and what they have learnt from it.

What can you and your coachees do to develop their capacity to encourage risk taking? Here's three exercises to practice to encourage risk-taking:

Exercise 1:
Role model risk-taking by using a GOOJF card or an «I messed up» message – people need to see that you are OK with failing and then sharing your failure and what you learnt from it

Exercise 2:
Practice stretching yourself and others outside of comfort zones through small steps: what stretch assignments can you give and to whom this upcoming week?

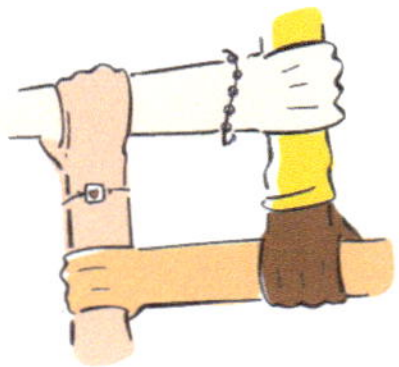

Exercise 3:
Share your desire to encourage risk-taking and ask your people for suggestions

Encourages Risk-taking: Coaching Questions

INDIVIDUAL LEVEL

1 Letting Go of Control:

- Can you describe a situation where you let go of control and allowed things to unfold naturally? What was the outcome?
- What fears or concerns do you have about relinquishing control, and how can you address them?

2 Stepping Outside Comfort Zones:

- What recent actions have you taken to step outside your comfort zone?
- How do you identify and pursue opportunities that challenge you to grow?

3 Creating Opportunities for Others:

- How have you created opportunities for others to shine and showcase their talents?
- Can you think of a time when you supported someone else in taking a risk? What was the result?

4 Supporting Others to Excel:

- How do you provide support and encouragement to others when they are taking risks?
- What strategies do you use to help others build their confidence and excel in challenging situations?

PROVIDING CONSTRUCTIVE CHALLENGE

Encourages Risk-taking: Coaching Questions

TEAM LEVEL

1. Letting Go of Control in Team:
   - How does your team practice distributing control and decision-making among its members?
   - What processes can your team implement to encourage more collaborative risk-taking?

2. Encouraging Team to Step Outside Comfort Zones:
   - How does your team create a culture where stepping outside comfort zones is encouraged and supported?
   - Can you share an example of a team project where taking risks led to significant growth or success?

3. Creating Opportunities for Team Members:
   - How do you identify and create opportunities for team members to showcase their skills and talents?
   - What initiatives can your team undertake to ensure everyone has a chance to lead and innovate?

4. Supporting Team Members to Excel:
   - How does your team support each other when facing challenges or taking risks?
   - What structures can your team put in place to provide ongoing support and encouragement for risk-taking?

Encourages Risk-taking: Coaching Questions

ORGANIZATIONAL LEVEL

1. **Organizational Culture of Letting Go of Control:**
   - How does your organization encourage leaders to let go of control and empower employees?
   - What policies or practices are in place to promote autonomy and distributed decision-making?

2. **Encouraging Risk-Taking at the Organizational Level:**
   - How does your organization foster an environment where employees feel safe to take risks and step outside their comfort zones?
   - What programs or initiatives can be introduced to support risk-taking and innovation across the organization?

3. **Creating Opportunities for Employees to Shine:**
   - How does your organization identify and create opportunities for employees to showcase their abilities and take on new challenges?
   - What recognition and reward systems are in place to celebrate those who take risks whether they fail or succeed?

4. **Supporting Employees to Excel:**
   - How does your organization provide support and resources for employees who are taking risks and striving to excel?
   - What mentorship or coaching programs can be developed to help employees build confidence and achieve their full potential?

PROVIDING CONSTRUCTIVE CHALLENGE

Inspires through Intrinsic Motivation

You will certainly remember someone in a professional context who has impressed you in a positive sense, who has been a secure base and both supported and stretched you to achieve more than you may have thought possible. Maybe it was a coach, a former manager or a colleague. These people remain in your memory for a long time - through what they said or did.

Secure base coachees inspire people through instilling a sense of purpose and meaning. When you ask people to talk about what has influenced and shaped them, their answers rarely include money or financial rewards. Instead, they make multiple references to people or events that helped them fulfill their potential, make a difference, contribute to a bigger purpose or gave them a passion for learning and development. If we look at Maslow's Hierarchy of needs, we see that once our basic needs are met, beyond a certain level, money becomes far less of a motivator in and of itself. People tend to be motivated by a sense that they are fulfilling their potential and helping others to fulfil theirs, too.

Ask your coachee, how might you develop your capacity to inspire through intrinsic motivation? Here's three exercises to practice as you continue to develop this characteristic:

Exercise 1:

Notice the words you use to inspire people when you speak: balance the focus on financial rewards, results and outcomes with a focus on learning, growth and development

Exercise 2:

Take time to get to know your people so that you have a better idea of what motivates them and what gives them meaning

Exercise 3:

Remember the two legs of acceptance and achievement: invite people to be part of something bigger than themselves. See how you can link day-to-day work to a larger purpose

PROVIDING CONSTRUCTIVE CHALLENGE

Inspires through Intrinsic Motivation: Coaching Questions

INDIVIDUAL LEVEL

1. **Self-Driven and Motivated:**
   - What activities or goals do you find most motivating and fulfilling?
   - How do you maintain your intrinsic motivation when facing obstacles or setbacks?

2. **Sense of Achievement:**
   - Can you share a recent accomplishment that gave you a strong sense of achievement? What made it meaningful to you?
   - How do you set and pursue goals that align with your intrinsic motivations and personal values?

3. **Desire to Make a Difference:**
   - What drives your desire to make a difference in your personal or professional life?
   - How do you ensure that your actions and decisions contribute to a greater purpose?

4. **Meaning and Purpose:**
   - How do you identify and align your work with your personal sense of meaning and purpose?
   - What strategies do you use to keep your purpose front and center in your daily activities?

Inspires through Intrinsic Motivation: Coaching Questions

TEAM LEVEL

1. **Leveraging Team Motivation:**
   - How does your team identify and harness the intrinsic motivations of its members?
   - What practices can your team implement to ensure everyone feels motivated and valued?

2. **Instilling a Sense of Achievement:**
   - How does your team celebrate achievements and milestones in a way that reinforces intrinsic motivation?
   - Can you share an example of a team accomplishment that was particularly meaningful and why?

3. **Making a Difference as a Team:**
   - How does your team ensure that its projects and goals are aligned with making a positive impact?
   - What initiatives can your team undertake to increase its contribution to a greater cause?

4. **Creating Meaning and Purpose:**
   - How does your team connect its work to a larger purpose or mission?
   - What can your team do to ensure that every member feels their work is meaningful and purposeful?

Inspires through Intrinsic Motivation: Coaching Questions

ORGANIZATIONAL LEVEL

1 Fostering Organizational Motivation:

- How does your organization identify and nurture the intrinsic motivations of its employees?
- What programs or initiatives can be introduced to support self-driven motivation across the organization?

2 Promoting a Sense of Achievement:

- How does your organization recognize and celebrate individual and team achievements in a way that fosters intrinsic motivation?
- What systems can be put in place to ensure employees feel a sense of accomplishment in their roles?

3 Encouraging a Desire to Make a Difference:

- How does your organization communicate its mission and values to inspire a desire to make a difference among employees?
- What opportunities are available for employees to contribute to meaningful projects or causes?

4 Aligning with Meaning and Purpose:

- How does your organization help employees align their work with their personal sense of meaning and purpose?
- What steps can be taken to ensure that the organization's goals and initiatives are perceived as meaningful by employees?

HAVING COURAGEOUS COMMUNICATION

The three characteristics that fall under the Courageous Communication category are Uses Listening and Inquiry, Delivers Powerful Messages and Signals Accessibility.

From a coaching perspective, supporting a coachee in developing courageous communication is crucial for their personal and professional growth. This process begins with the coach employing listening and inquiry techniques, ensuring they practice active listening to fully understand and engage with the coachee's perspectives and concerns. By modeling and encouraging clear and powerful messaging, coaches help coachees articulate their thoughts and ideas in a way that resonates and drives impact. Additionally, signaling accessibility by being mentally available and responding within a reasonable timeframe demonstrates respect and builds trust. This holistic approach to communication fosters an environment where the coachee feels empowered to speak honestly and confidently, tackling difficult conversations and advocating for themselves effectively. Through this supportive dynamic, coachees learn to navigate their interactions with courage and clarity, ultimately enhancing their ability to lead and collaborate.

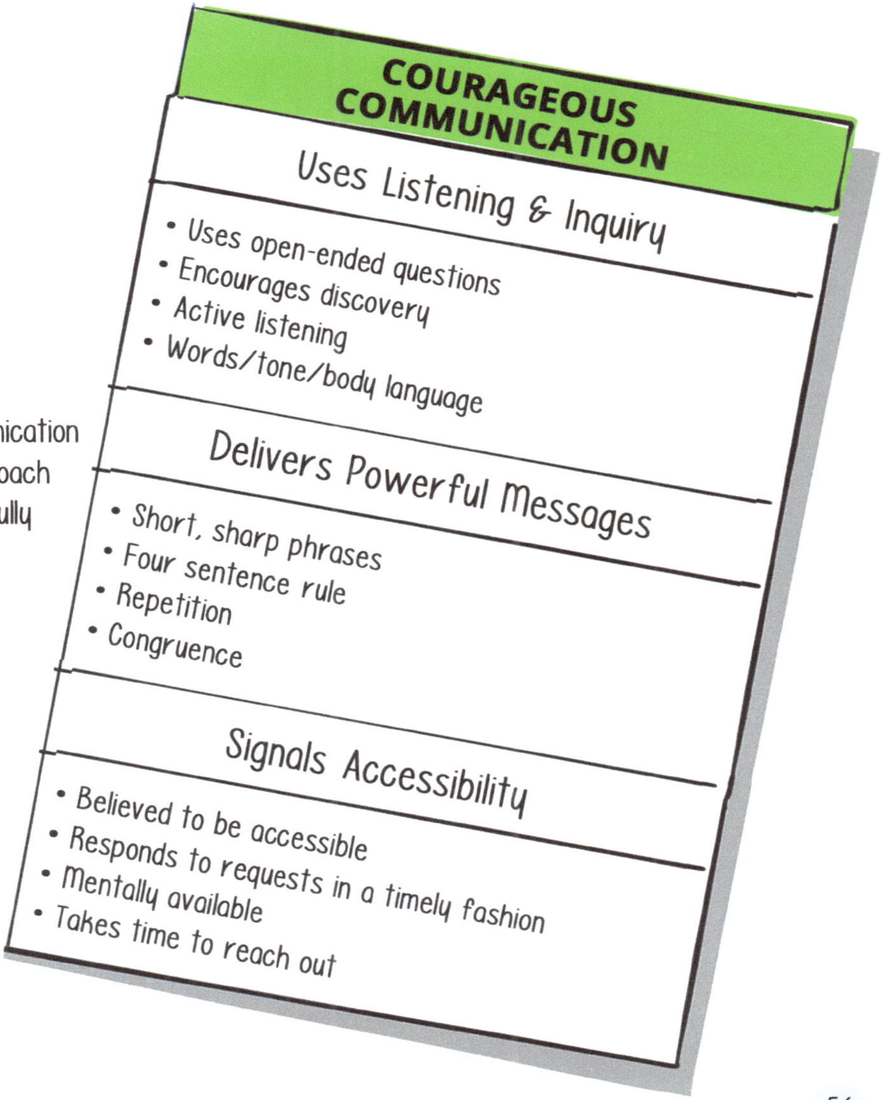

HAVING COURAGEOUS COMMUNICATION

Uses Listening and Inquiry

This is often the characteristic with which most leaders struggle. However, it is only natural that we find this characteristic challenging. Our brain thinks at least four times faster than someone can speak, and so whilst the other person talks, we're often running ahead in our brains. By practising the techniques to actively listen & inquire you will find that small daily gestures can make a significant difference.

Many leaders feel they are there to provide the solution as quickly and efficiently as possible.
However, by asking questions, you encourage others to co-create with you, to find the answers themselves and thus to expand their potential and engagement.

Human beings have a basic need to be heard. Secure bases are able to provide a space where a person truly feels listened to — this is often one of the greatest gifts we can give each other. In the words of Professor Bill Fischer, "Be interested versus interesting."

So how can you support your coachee to improve their listening & inquiry skills? Here are three exercises to develop this capacity:

Exercise 1:

Practice active listening: be aware of the other person's tone, body language and the feeling as well as the words themselves

Exercise 2:

Use open-ended questions: Who, what, when, where, how questions to stimulate dialogue

Exercise 3:

Practice getting comfortable with the power of the pause: after speaking, allow the other person the space and time to reflect and respond.
Avoid rushing to fill the silence.

Uses Listening and Inquiry: Coaching Questions

INDIVIDUAL LEVEL

1 Using Open-Ended Questions:

- How do you typically formulate your questions when seeking information or understanding from others?
- Can you provide an example of a time when using open-ended questions led to a deeper and more meaningful conversation?

2 Practicing Active Listening:

- How do you ensure that you are fully present and attentive when someone is speaking to you?
- What techniques do you use to demonstrate that you are actively listening to the speaker?

3 Encouraging Discovery:

- How do you create an environment that encourages others to share their thoughts and ideas openly?
- Can you recall a situation where your listening and inquiry skills helped someone else discover a new perspective or solution?

4 Being Conscious of Words, Tone, and Body Language:

- How aware are you of your words, tone, and body language during conversations? How do you think they impact the interaction?
- What steps do you take to ensure your non-verbal communication aligns with your verbal messages?

Uses Listening and Inquiry: Coaching Questions

TEAM LEVEL

1 Using Open-Ended Questions in Team Settings:

- How does your team utilize open-ended questions to foster collaboration and innovation?
- What can your team do to improve the use of open-ended questions during meetings and discussions?

2 Practicing Active Listening in Teams:

- How does your team practice active listening during discussions and decision-making processes?
- What practices can be implemented to enhance active listening skills within the team?

3 Encouraging Discovery Among Team Members:

- How does your team create a culture that encourages the exploration of new ideas and perspectives?
- Can you share an example of a team project where active listening and inquiry led to significant discoveries or breakthroughs?

4 Conscious Communication in Teams:

- How does your team ensure that words, tone, and body language are consistent and supportive during interactions?
- What training or initiatives can your team undertake to improve overall communication skills?

Uses Listening and Inquiry: Coaching Questions

ORGANIZATIONAL LEVEL

1. **Promoting Open-Ended Questions Organization-Wide:**
   - How does your organization encourage the use of open-ended questions to drive innovation and problem-solving?
   - What initiatives can be introduced to train employees on the importance and use of open-ended questions?

2. **Fostering a Culture of Active Listening:**
   - How does your organization promote active listening as a core value?
   - What programs or workshops can be implemented to enhance active listening skills across the organization?

3. **Encouraging Organizational Discovery:**
   - How does your organization create an environment where employees feel safe to share their ideas and explore new possibilities?
   - Can you provide examples of how listening and inquiry have led to significant organizational improvements or innovations?

4. **Ensuring Conscious Communication:**
   - How does your organization train employees to be mindful of their words, tone, and body language?
   - What steps can be taken to ensure that all forms of communication within the organization are effective and aligned with its values?

Delivers Powerful Messages

One common theme we often hear from employees relates to a lack of clear and consistent communication. What you share – the content – is important but equally important, if not more so, is the 'how' you communicate. To motivate people, it is important to communicate key messages in a way that appeals to the head (information), heart (inspiration), and hands (involvement). Remember, facts prove while stories move: storytelling is a powerful way to communicate memorably. Short belief statements or phrases of support can make a significant difference. Words have the power to demoralize as well as inspire people. In fact, many executives are easily able to recall words or stories that resonated with them decades later.

How can you support your coachees in delivering powerful messages? Try these three exercises for this characteristic:

Exercise 1:

Practice using the four-sentence rule this week. Speak succinctly then ask a question to create dialogue

Exercise 2:

Practice using short stories and condensing what you want to say into a maximum of three key points that stimulate curiosity and interest

Exercise 3:

Reflect on your non-verbal signals – play with varying your tone and use gestures appropriate to the message

Delivers Powerful Messages: Coaching Questions

1. ## Using Short Memorable Phrases:
   - Can you share an example of a short, memorable phrase you've used effectively in communication? What made it impactful?
   - How do you create and integrate memorable phrases into your daily communication to enhance your messages?

2. ## Applying the Four Sentence Rule:
   - How do you ensure your messages are concise and to the point? Have you used the four sentence rule in your communications?
   - Can you identify a situation where following the four sentence rule improved the clarity and impact of your message?

3. ## Repetition and Consistency:
   - How do you ensure that your key messages are consistently communicated across different contexts and conversations?
   - What strategies do you use to reinforce important messages through repetition without sounding redundant?

4. ## Displaying Congruence:
   - How do you ensure that there is alignment between your words, tone, body language, and actions?
   - Can you provide an example of a time when your congruence in communication led to increased trust or credibility with others?

HAVING COURAGEOUS COMMUNICATION

TEAM LEVEL

1. Using Short Memorable Phrases in Teams:
   - How does your team develop and use short, memorable phrases to reinforce key messages and values?
   - What are some effective phrases your team has used to drive home important points or initiatives?

2. Applying the Four Sentence Rule in Team Settings:
   - How can your team implement the four sentence rule to improve the efficiency and clarity of your meetings and discussions?
   - Can you share an example of a team discussion where concise communication led to better understanding and decision-making?

3. Repetition and Consistency in Team Communication:
   - How does your team ensure that key messages are repeated and reinforced consistently across different channels and interactions?
   - What methods can your team use to track and maintain message consistency over time?

4. Displaying Congruence in Team Actions:
   - How does your team ensure that its actions are aligned with the messages it communicates?
   - What practices can your team adopt to regularly assess and improve the congruence between words,

Delivers Powerful Messages: Coaching Questions

ORGANIZATIONAL LEVEL

1. Using Short Memorable Phrases Organizationally:
   - How does your organization develop and use short, memorable phrases to communicate its vision, mission, and values?
   - What are some key phrases that have become part of the organizational culture and why are they effective?

2. Applying the Four Sentence Rule Organization-Wide:
   - How can your organization promote the use of the four sentence rule to improve communication across all levels?
   - What training or resources can be provided to help employees communicate more concisely and effectively?

3. Repetition and Consistency in Organizational Messages:
   - How does your organization ensure that key messages are repeated and reinforced consistently across all communication platforms?
   - What systems or processes are in place to monitor and maintain message consistency throughout the organization?

4. Displaying Congruence Organizationally:
   - How does your organization ensure that its actions are in line with its communicated messages and values?
   - What steps can be taken to regularly review and enhance the congruence between what the organization says and what it does?

Signals Accessibility

Accessibility does not require a physical presence – rather it is about fostering focused attention.

it's important to stress that signalling accessibility does not mean that you are available 24/7. What matters is that people believe that if they reach out, they'll be heard and responded to within a reasonable timeframe. The idea of being accessible is less about the amount or frequency of contact time and more about the perception of the relationship. You become a secure base through your perceived availability in a time of need.
If it helps, you can think of accessibility as an 'invisible' aspect of being a secure base in that you are 'present' with the person even when you are not there. This can even be true of people who are no longer alive; they can be accessed through memory and thus remain a secure base for you long after their physical presence has passed on. Olympic coach Jack Queen, now deceased, once gave me a card that I treasure, where he wrote "If you feel downhearted or exhilarated go stand in the sunlight and look at your shadow – that's my hand on your shoulder."

What can be done to develop the ability to signal accessibility? Here's three exercises that a coachee can practice:

Exercise 1:

Arrive 5mins early for meetings/remote calls and/or stay 5mins after.
Check in over physical/virtual teas/coffees.

Exercise 2:

Send occasional text messages, handwritten notes or emails with short messages to demonstrate that people are in your thoughts and to express appreciation

Exercise 3:

Practice focusing fully on the person when you are speaking with them, putting aside other distractions

Signals Accessibility: Coaching Questions

1. Believed to be Accessible and Responsive:
   - How do you ensure that others perceive you as accessible and responsive in your personal and professional interactions?
   - Can you recall a time when someone expressed appreciation for your accessibility? What did you do that made them feel this way?

2. Responding within a Reasonable Timeframe:
   - What strategies do you use to manage your time and ensure you respond to communications promptly?
   - How do you balance the need to respond quickly with the importance of providing thoughtful and complete responses?

3. Being Mentally Available:
   - How do you practice being fully present and mentally available when interacting with others?
   - What techniques help you minimize distractions and focus on the person you are with?

4. Taking Time to Connect:
   - How often do you proactively reach out to connect with others, both personally and professionally?
   - What are some ways you can improve your efforts to connect and build relationships with those around you?

Signals Accessibility: Coaching Questions

TEAM LEVEL

1. Team Perception of Accessibility:
   - How does your team ensure that all members feel accessible and responsive to each other's needs?
   - What can your team do to foster an environment where accessibility is a shared value and practice?

2. Team Response Time:
   - How does your team manage communication to ensure timely responses to each other and external stakeholders?
   - What processes can your team put in place to improve response times without compromising the quality of interactions?

3. Mental Availability in Team Interactions:
   - How does your team encourage members to be mentally present and fully engaged during meetings and collaborative efforts?
   - What practices can your team adopt to reduce distractions and enhance focus during team interactions?

4. Proactive Team Connections:
   - How does your team make time to connect and build relationships beyond immediate work tasks?
   - What activities or initiatives can your team implement to strengthen connections and foster a sense of community?

Signals Accessibility: Coaching Questions

ORGANIZATIONAL LEVEL

1. Organizational Culture of Accessibility:
   - How does your organization promote a culture where accessibility and responsiveness are prioritized?
   - What measures can your organization take to ensure leaders and employees are perceived as accessible?

2. Organizational Response Practices:
   - How does your organization ensure that communications are responded to within a reasonable timeframe?
   - What systems or tools can be implemented to help employees manage and improve response times?

3. Mental Availability Across the Organization:
   - How does your organization support employees in being mentally available and fully present in their interactions?
   - What training or resources can be provided to help employees improve their focus and presence during work?

4. Encouraging Organizational Connections:
   - How does your organization encourage leaders and employees to take time to connect and build relationships?
   - What programs or initiatives can be introduced to foster stronger connections and a sense of community within the organization?

HOW CAN I COACH FOR SELF-ASSESSMENT ON THE SECURE BASE CHARACTERISTICS?

CONSCIOUS CHOICE	CONSTRUCTIVE CHALLENGE	COURAGEOUS COMMUNICATION
Stays Calm	**Sees the Potential**	**Uses Listening & Inquiry**
• Mindfulness • Four deep breaths • Keeps perpective • Leads others	• Believes in potential to develop • Growth versus fixed mindset • Stretches & challenges the individual • Statements of belief	• Uses open-ended questions • Encourages discovery • Active listening • Words/tone/body language
Accepts the Individual	**Encourages Risk-taking**	**Delivers Powerful Messages**
• Unconditional positive regard • I'm ok, you're ok • Separates the person from the problem • Collective consciousness	• Confidence to let go of control • Focuses self and others on stepping out of comfort zones • Creates opportunities for others to shine • Supports others to excel	• Short, sharp phrases • Four sentence rule • Repetition • Congruence
Focuses on the Positive	**Inspires through Intrinsic Motivation**	**Signals Accessibility**
• Looks for the learning • Switches from negative to positive • Sells the benefits of pain • Helps others to see the positive	• Self-driven & motivated • Instills a sense of achievement • Desire to 'make a difference' somehow • Leverages the power of the team	• Believed to be accessible • Responds to requests in a timely fashion • Mentally available • Takes time to reach out

HOW CAN I COACH FOR SELF-ASSESSMENT ON THE SECURE BASE CHARACTERISTICS?

The secure base coach can use the Secure Base Wheel to ask the coachee to self-assess on the three categories and nine characteristics. Based on the responses, the coach can then use the coaching questions to explore further what the coachee would like to focus on and what actions they might like to take. Coachees can also use this tool as a 360 by asking their boss, peers, direct reports and other colleagues to complete the wheel for them and then have an open dialogue around the responses. For an electronic AI assisted version, coaches can use the 100 facets tool (see relevant resources section).

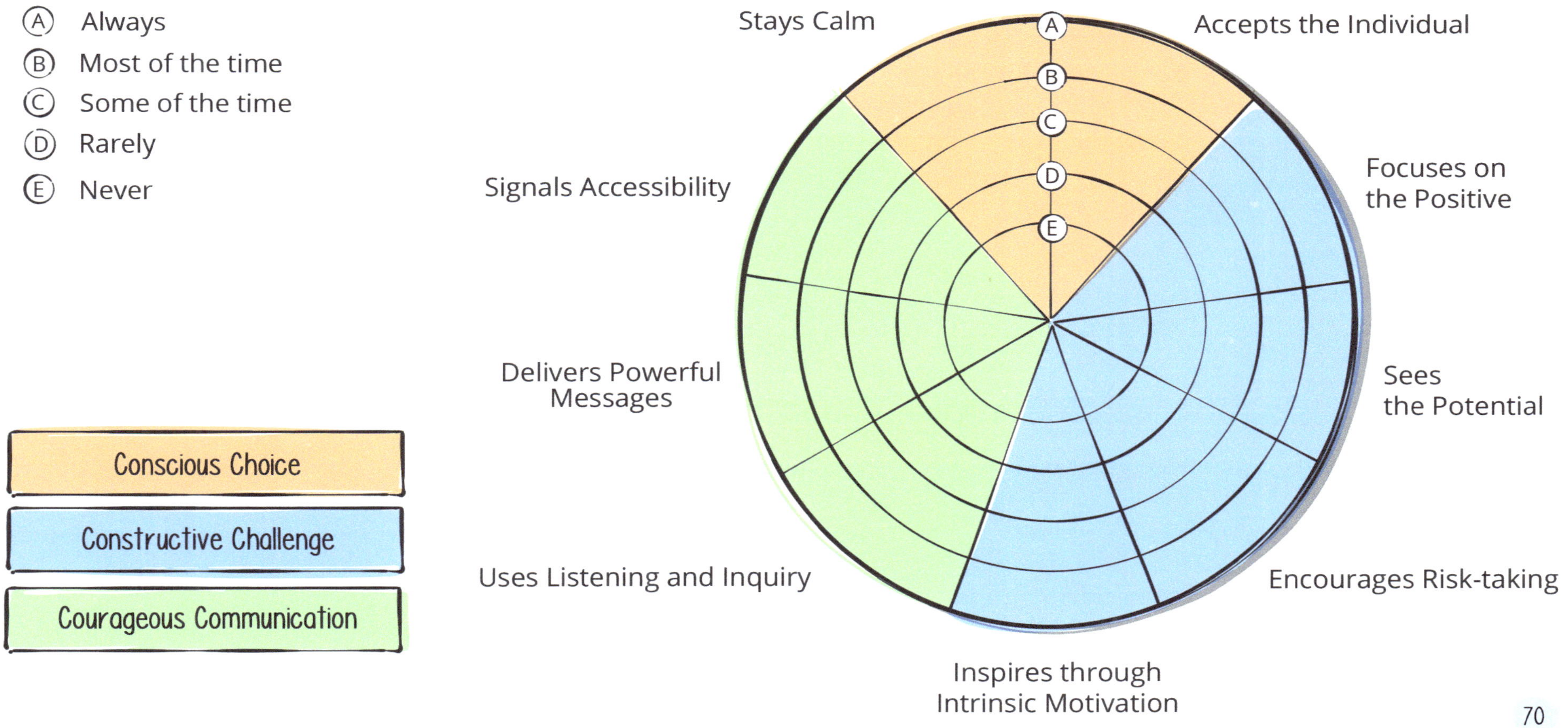

WHAT ARE THE REFERENCES AND SOME RELEVANT RESOURCES?

References:

- Care to Dare: Unleashing astonishing potential through secure base leadership (2012)
  By Kohlreiser, Goldsworthy & Coombe, published by Jossey Bass, an imprint of Wiley & sons.

Relevant Resources:

- 100 facets - Secure Base assessment 360 tool:
  https://100facets.ai/topics/666fede56b96f136a7564c31/
- Secure Base Leadership Characteristics Video Series: 11 short videos with short exercises: contact IMD
- The Craft of the Secure Base Coach: Enabling Transition (2024)
  https://www.routledge.com/The-Craft-of-the-Secure-Base-Coach-Enabling-Transition
  vanWielink-vanGasteren-Reimerink-Verbokkem-Oerlemans-Wilhelm-Fiddelaers-Jaspers
  p/book/9781032701233
- On becoming a person: a therapists view of psychotherapy (1961) by Carl R. Rogers, published by Houghton Miffl Company
- Way of Being (1995) by Carl R. Rogers, published by Houghton Mifflin Company
- Person-centred Counselling in Action (2013) Fourth Edition by Means, Thorne & McLeod, published by Sage Publications.

WHO DO I WANT TO ACKNOWLEDGE ?

Gratitude to Sébastien Gerbier for his outstanding layout and illustrations : it has been a joy to collaborate.

Much gratitude to my co-authors of Care to Dare: George Kohlrieser and Duncan Coombe for the research, insights and exploration in bringing the secure base concept into the business world.
Gratitude to ALPIQ & ROBECO for having the courage to transform their cultures from within, applying the secure base principles and training executives as secure base coaching ambassadors.

Gratitude to all the secure base coaches and executives I am privileged to know and learn from, with special mention to those who contributed quotes to this playbook.
Gratitude to Eivind Slaaen, whose secure base intervention prompted the creation of this playbook..
Gratitude to Erick Rinner who inspires a calm, cosmic compassion on a daily basis.

Thank you to all the participants (past and present) of the IMD IECC Coaching Certificate Program as well as my co-program directors, Silke Mischke and Severine Jourdain, our program advisor, Diego Goehring, our program co-ordinator, Kamila Kosmala, my program assistant, Teresa Virseda, our logistics and facilities maestro, Hervé De Conchy, our Maitre D, Clement Plaza and everyone else involved- we all challenge what is and inspire what could be together for the potential benefit of people and planet.

WHO'S BEHIND THIS PLAYBOOK ?

About the Author: Rev. Dr. Susan Goldsworthy OLY

Susan Goldsworthy is an Affiliate Professor of Leadership, Communications and Organizational Change at IMD. An Olympic finalist, award-winning author, C-suite executive coach, and speaker with more than 20 years of corporate experience in large multinationals, Susan brings knowledge from the fields of sport, business, neuroscience and spirituality to her leadership development. In an increasingly uncertain world, she emphasizes activating awareness, accountability and agency by cultivating spiritual wellbeing and secure-base-spaces. She works with individuals, teams and companies to co-create the conditions for healthy, healing and sustainable high performance. Ordained as a OneSpirit Interfaith Minister, Susan holds a PhD in Organizational Change from Hult Ashridge, a Masters in Coaching & Consulting for Change from HEC/Oxford, an Executive Masters in the Neuroscience of Leadership from Middlesex University/NLI, and the Certificate in Coaching for Leadership from the Tavistock Institute. She is also trained as a breathwork practitioner and in the use of numerous psychometric assessment tools. Susan is Co-Director of IMD's Executive Coaching Certificate, Director of IMD's Leading Sustainable Change program and CEO of Goldswolf & Associates. She seeks to balance the brutal beauty of being with the daily discipline of doing to benefit all of livingkind. Through secure base coaching she believes we can reconnect to our shared humanity.

About the Illustrator: Sebastien Gerbier

Sebastien Gerbier holds a degree in industrial design and spent a decade working as a designer in Paris, Senegal and Mali. After returning to his hometown of Annecy (France) in 2012, he founded a drawing class workshop to teach academic drawing. He aims to give his students the opportunity to discover and fine-tune their own capabilities and skills, supporting them to dare to be creative.

Sebastien is a graphic facilitator and designer for several corporate clients including: L'Oreal, Lego, IMD, Renault, Medtronic, Nestle, Sophia Genetics, SNCF... He illustrates values, strategic visions and projects during innovation programs.

PRAISE FOR SECURE BASE COACHING

I have used many leadership coaching frameworks, and I found the secure base coaching model uniquely powerful as it quickly clarifies practical steps that one can act on, and improve in. It is sophisticated with 9 behaviours that really hit on the key leadership challenges, yet easy to use and understand both for coaches and the coachees, which makes it super powerful for deep discussions. With Dr. Goldsworthy's immense wealth of experience from helping thousands of executives thrive, this guide is truly empowering for coaches who want to make an impact at a world-class level.

Dr. Mohamad Razaghi ,
Award winning leadership-tech entrepreneur,
coach, keynote speaker

To truly thrive, we must care for others with genuine compassion, dare to step beyond our comfort zones in pursuit of growth, and share our resources generously. By doing so, we build more connected and supportive relationships, unlocking our clients' potential and bringing out their best. When tapping into this, we use our superpower as coaches.

Angelica Adamski,
CEO, Board Director and Senior Executive Coach

Intentionally showing up as a safe leader, discerning when to care and when to dare, cultivates an environment that maximizes human potential. Moreover, being a safe leader is not just advantageous for others; it significantly benefits the leader. One must develop a secure relationship with oneself to effectively provide safety for others.

Tony Jamous
CEO OysterHR

PRAISE FOR SECURE BASE COACHING

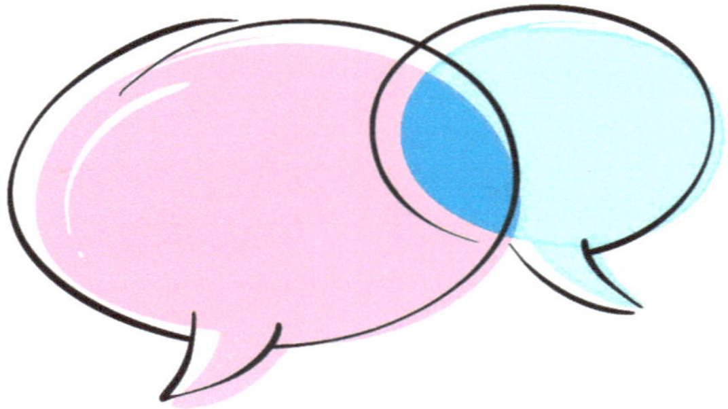

The Care-Dare-Share philosophy is at the heart of Alpiq. We won't succeed in enabling a better climate and an improved security of supply just by ourselves. Which is why our company's purpose starts with the simple word 'Together'. Being rooted in caring, daring, and sharing helps us move past traditional notions of heroic leadership towards a much more human-centered, trust-based approach - essential in today's increasingly complex and uncertain business environment.

Simon Reber
Head Organizational Development
and Leadership, ALPIQ

Secure base leadership as the IMD philosophy is for me a life-changing event, both professionally and personally, because it provides insight into how powerful a secure base is, which secure bases (not only humans) you have & cherish and for whom you are a secure base. Having one or hopefully more secures bases is crucial as an inspirational and safe haven to develop and challenge yourself in this increasingly complex world that has higher expectations and therefore creates more pressure and stress

Robin van Wankum,
Owner, SPOT-on

Secure base coaching creates the conditions of psychological safety to empower the coachee to go, with confidence and a touch of bravery, far beyond their comfort zone to find their own way.

Diego Piovan, Managing Partner Hermes Consulting

PRAISE FOR SECURE BASE COACHING

By fostering a secure base, we empower individuals and teams to explore their potential with courage, resilience and hope. When we provide unwavering support and trust, we ignite a profound transition that transcends challenges and cultivates enduring growth. The true essence of coaching lies in creating this foundation of safety from which people can reach new heights. Leaders and coaches that learn to be a secure base are miracle workers!

Jakob Van Weilink
Partner, The School for Transition
Leadership coach & trainer at the Portland Institute for Loss and Transition

This Secure Base Coach Playbook is packed full of exercises and questions to support coaches and coachees to deepen connections and heighten performance in service of a healthier way of being.

Robyn Renaud
Founder, Forward Bound, C-suite Executive Coach, Horse Coach

Secure Base Coaching is a powerful yet accessible tool to boost performance while prioritizing human connection. This approach revolutionizes teamwork by combining empathy and strategic thinking. This playbook supports coaches, coachees and executives to care, dare and share together.

Pascal Chauvie
Leadership Coach, Juan-Pascal Coaching

PRAISE FOR SECURE BASE COACHING

In my leadership coaching, I value the secure base approach to balance support with challenge, allowing for the expression of vulnerability, which supports deeper understanding and leads to personal growth.

Rolf Frey, MSc
Managing Partner, DOMINÉ & PARTNERS LTD. & C-Suite Coach

With conscious intention to BOTH care AND dare, Secure Base Coaching helps to create a safe space to grow together. When we challenge ourselves and others with empathy and curiosity, we can reach deeper levels of honesty, awareness and psychological safety. In this space, there is the possibility to truly "see" ourselves and others and to connect as human beings.

Jennie Zeiner
Executive Coach & Learning Manager

Secure base coaching is essential to maximise growth and development and increase self awareness. The concept of caring and daring is such a wonderful way to create psychological safety and to challenge a coachee to unexplored areas and depth that one would never have imagined. I would say it's the foundation of impactful coaching.

Richard Westbroek
CEO & Founder, ChamoiX Coaching

PRAISE FOR SECURE BASE COACHING

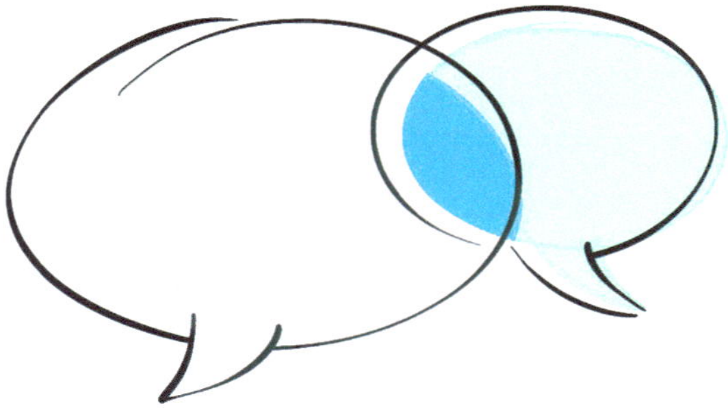

Secure base coaching means caring & daring, supporting & challenging to unleash each and every client's potential and enabling them to find their own way to thrive.

Willem Jan Hofmans, DBA, PCC
Leadership & C-suite Coach

Secure base coaching involves fostering the clients' experience of autonomy and freedom of choice (however limited the choices might appear). Discovering the connection of prior-to-now life experiences and here-and-now emotional and behavioral patterns is a reliable entry-point to free oneself to new emotional and behavioral responses.

Andreas Phileas Neumann
Senior Facilitator for Organizational Development

Secure Base Coaching is anchored in a deep caring relationship between the coach and the coachee that steers clear from dependence or rescuing. This caring relationship represents an opportunity for daring such as constructive challenge of limiting beliefs and unhelpful patterns. It also encourages exploration and risk-taking from a place of connection and deep psychological safety. I believe that Secure Base coaching exemplifies the power of transformative coaching in a way I have never seen before encouraging both the coach and the coachee to care and dare for each other.

Michela Andrenacci,
Leadership Consultant & C-Suite Coach

PRAISE FOR SECURE BASE COACHING

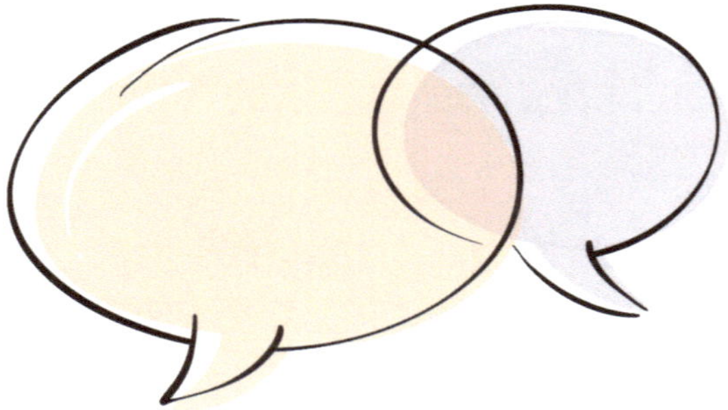

The SBL-philosophy inspires you to reflect on, to revise and to activate your unique coaching and leadership-style. It helps you to launch yourself to grow as a partner, parent, coach and leader.

Patrick Spits
Founder & Owner, Spits Activates

Secure base coaching is about being truly listened to and building a foundation of trust where the unspoken can be voiced. It taps into authenticity and encourages taking responsibility for one's behavior. By understanding our emotional landscape, we build resilience and create space for calm reflection, allowing clarity to emerge. With emotional awareness and a clear mind, we gain a solid base to enhance the effectiveness of our actions.

Igor Dimnik
VP Product, SITA

Secure Base Coaching is an impactful approach that is created through a meaningful connection that incorporates sharing, caring and daring between the coach and coachee. By working together, they use the insights to then challenge, inspire, encourage and dare the coachee to stretch beyond where they currently are into their "zone of promise and potential" and ultimately achieve their own incredible developmental results.

Rebecca Meadows
Senior Executive Leadership Coach

www.ingramcontent.com/pod-product-compliance
Lightning Source LLC
LaVergne TN
LVHW061735220125
801884LV00009B/70
9782940485772